The Road to Class A Manufacturing Resource Planning — MRP II

The Road to Class A Manufacturing Resource Planning — MRP II

*What every senior manager, project manager and
project team leader needs to know to ensure
a successful new business system implementation.*

Michael G. Tincher and Donald H. Sheldon

Buker, Inc. *Chicago Boston
Kansas City Salt Lake City
Johannesburg London
Mexico City Sydney*

·BUKER·

© 1995 Buker, Inc.
Second Printing-1997
All rights reserved. Published 1997
Printed in the United States of America
01 00 99 98 97 96 95   5 4 3 2 1

ISBN 1-57512-003-8

This book is printed on acid-free paper.

Contents

Preface

A great deal of material has been written in recent years about process improvement and continuous improvement in general. Buker, Inc. has had the privilege of working with hundreds of firms as they have taken on the challenging job of remaining competitive in increasingly global markets. Our experience at Buker, Inc. has consistently shown common threads woven into the fabric of each of these journeys of process improvement. Within the theory of Manufacturing Resource Planning (MRP II), developed several years ago, lies the premise that improvement starts with understanding your business. Manufacturing Resource Planning (MRP II) implemented correctly with the latest understanding of organizational behavior and quality standards that meet and exceed the requirements of the customer and supported with performance measurements that flex with changing need, constitutes the fundamental improvement process that World Class businesses require today. Companies may call their improvement initiatives Manufacturing Resource Planning (MRP II), Total Quality (TQ), Just-In-Time (JIT), Business Re-Engineering, or World Class, but the important thing is to utilize all of the relevant techniques and resources. With today's competitive nature of world commerce, businesses must use all of the knowledge and talent available. This means that pure Manufacturing Resource Planning (MRP II) implementations are rare. What we see, instead, are hybrid implementations tailored to meet each firm's requirements and weaknesses. Manufacturing Resource Planning (MRP II), in its purest form, creates a stability within the business which allows continuous improvement to flourish. When linked with the additional improvement elements of Total Quality (TQ) and Just-In-Time (JIT), a firm can condense the implementation cycle time and achieve significant bottom line return in a fraction of the time that would have been required only a few years ago.

This book is targeted at eliminating some of the misconceptions surrounding the foundation of process improvement and to reassure you that process improvement yields great bounty. It is authored by Michael G. Tincher, the president of Buker, Inc, and an educator and business consultant, along with Donald H. Sheldon, a practitioner with top management experience, who has successfully managed a Class A implementation as a project leader while a client of Buker's. The book is designed and offered as an up-to-date resource on the theory and objectives of Manufacturing Resource Planning (MRP II). If you are contemplating an improvement process in your firm, this book will help you understand the basics in simple modern terms. We think it is important to understand these basics. It is difficult to build a strong house on a weak foundation. Manufacturing Resource Planning (MRP II) can provide that strong foundation.

Acknowledgements

Anne Cobb, Empire State College, State University of New York, Saratoga Springs, New York.

CHAPTER 1

What is Manufacturing Resource Planning?

Starting this book, we sit in our offices surrounded by books about improvement processes. These books offer techniques and theories, complex and simple, but something still seems to be missing. Many of these books assume too much as they begin to tell their readers of the techniques of the journey to excellence. These books often take a rather technical, textbook approach. The objective of this book is to address the real issues behind the need for, expectations, and implementation of Manufacturing Resource Planning (MRP II).

The roots of Manufacturing Resource Planning (MRP II) started in the late 1960s and early 1970s with the use of computers and computer systems in manufacturing companies. The application of the computer as a tool to manipulate and store data began in the finance area. The initial application in finance was to use the computer to reduce manual record keeping and filing systems for payables, receivables, general ledger and payroll.

The logical progression of the computer as a tool to help run the business was to apply the computer resource to the operations side of the business, specifically to help plan, schedule and order material. This was called Material Requirements Planning (MRP).

In the 1970s, when computers became affordable for almost all businesses, thousands of companies began Material Requirements Planning (MRP) implementations. This was the decade of the MRP crusades. Companies rushed to implement this new tool to help manage inventories, improve material shortage conditions on the factory floor, reduce purchasing costs and improve on-time customer delivery.

At this time Material Requirements Planning (MRP) was viewed by the management of these companies as a computer tool. Involvement in the Material Requirements Planning (MRP) implementation normally was confined to planning and scheduling, information systems, finance, and manufacturing. Senior management did not view these new tools as a way to run the business and there was very little involvement from the other key business functions. For example, sales, engineering and quality saw very little need to actually participate in computer-based planning and scheduling systems. These systems were viewed simply as tools to help materials and manufacturing do their jobs.

MRP II

As more companies began to implement and use Material Requirements Planning (MRP) to help plan, schedule and order material a select few companies began to realize that to yield the full benefit of MRP, it must be viewed and managed as a total company operating system. This meant that all functions in the business, including those that previously had little involvement — senior management, sales, engineering, finance and quality — now began to utilize these tools as a way to help manage their operations.

This second generation of MRP now known as MRP II — Manufacturing Resource Planning — a method to effectively manage the total resources in a business enterprise, has evolved into one of the fundamental tools that many high performance businesses use today. The business view or model we will utilize to depict Manufacturing Resource Planning (MRP II) is shown in Figure 1-1.

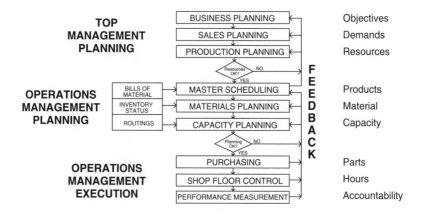

Figure 1-1: Business Model

Manufacturing Resource Planning (MRP II) is a structured approach, a process way of thinking, and a formal way to manage a manufacturing company. It is a process designed to help an organization get fundamental control of their business. The principles behind MRP II structure business habits. MRP II starts with top management planning. Having senior management engaged in directing the business operations through MRP II is fundamental to its success.

Business Plan

The element of MRP II where senior management states the overall objectives for the company is the *business plan*. The business plan includes the mission, direction, values, global goals and business imperatives of the company. Without a cohesive statement of goals and objectives, businesses may drift from their original vision without thought or planning. What may have started out as a vision to produce a product to meet a specific need many times ends up as a particular narrower focus within that vision. This is usually because one product or group of products surfaces as easier to sell than others. These companies with their lack of global market understanding find out too late that the original vision was lost and that someone else has moved in on their territory.

On the other side of the spectrum are companies that channel too much energy toward an unreviewed charter and find themselves in trouble. Sears' catalog business is such an example. Sears was very successful for decades with its core catalog business but did not review it in terms of changing market needs. While others were entering the catalog market successfully, the "old expert" was losing money where it once was the dominant force.

No one, least of all in a book, can tell you what the right product or focus is for your business. Making that decision is what risk and entrepreneurial spirit is all about. Being wrong is one thing, but not reviewing the basic questions is not understanding your reason for being in business. Additionally, if you expect others within your business to support and help you reach your goal, that goal must be clearly understood by all. Without defining the strategy, do not expect your employees to act out your script consistently. Do not underestimate the importance that a common set of goals and objectives brings to the organization. MRP II is hierarchical. It flows directly from the goals and objectives stated in the business plan.

One of the initial ways to involve senior management directly in the MRP II initiative is through the development of a comprehensive business planning process. This process engages senior management in the discussion and confirmation of strategic intentions for the business resources.

Sales Plan

From the business plan, the next step in the Manufacturing Resource Planning (MRP II) process is the *sales plan*. The sales plan is a statement of demand — what the company intends to sell. This plan is developed for each product line or product family. It is stated in both dollars and units of measure and normally extends 12 months into the future. The sales plan sets the drum beat for manufacturing with forecasts of the rate of demand and product mix for each product family. Many decisions are made more accurately in the business when a process of review and revision of the sales plan takes place.

Decisions that are communicated in the business plan should be made with great understanding of the market and a conscious calculation of risk. For example, if top management decides that an existing technology is short-lived and that another avenue pursued would provide better potential for the company, then resources must be aligned to move in that direction. Sales and marketing strategies, pricing, distribution, promotional strategies and product design specifications must reflect the changing objectives being stated in the business plan.

Production Plan

From the business and sales plans, plans now can be made which define the required manufacturing resources. Manufacturing strategies, already stated in the business plan, provide management input in the development of order backlog plans for make to order products and inventory plans for make to stock products. This management input becomes the basis for the *production plan* development. Production planning is quite easy to accomplish when there is a business plan and sales plan in place. The linking of the top management planning elements of business planning, sales planning and production planning are depicted below.

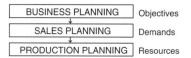

Figure 1-2: Top Management Planning

The production plan is a document that states resource requirements by product family or line. Like the sales plan, it normally extends 12 months into the future. It is top management's determination of how to respond to the marketplace demands anticipated in the sales plan. The communication loop is important here. Inability to meet manufacturing capacity requirements would be assessed and fed back to the sales plan. A top management decision would result in changes to either the sales plan, the production plan (in terms of additional capital, etc.), or even the business plan itself may require

5

change. Too many companies create unrealistic sales and revenue plans with no proactive plan to actually produce the product, even if the sales did materialize.

To prevent this from occurring, high performance companies develop a monthly operations review at the senior management level. This is sometimes called the sales and operations planning process. The monthly review by senior management provides a structured approach to align each product family production rate to the changing marketplace demand.

Production Planning Objectives

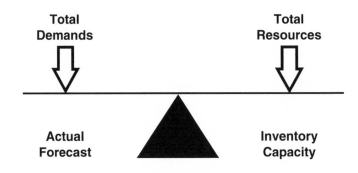

Total Demands

Total Resources

Actual Forecast

Inventory Capacity

Allocate Company Resources to Capitalize on the "Best" Marketplace Opportunities

Figure 1-3: Production Planning Objectives

The production plan, therefore, links strategic goals to production and is coordinated with sales objectives, resource availabilities, and financial budgets. If the production plan is not integrated, production managers cannot be held responsible for meeting the plan, and informal approaches will develop to overcome inconsistencies. (Vollman et al., 363)

The production plan is missing in many companies. In the past it had been assumed that capacity either was always available or could be added quickly. The skill set required in today's more sophisticated workplace does not always efficiently lend itself to significant demand swings. Skills required for computer-operated, operator-programmed machinery often takes months of intensive training and/or experience. In the days of hand-operated, labor intensive operations, it was expected that labor could be added quickly. Regardless of the past, effective production planning is required today because acute competition forces the need for optimal performance.

These three top level plans — business plan, sales plan, and production plan — make up the TOP MANAGEMENT PLANNING portion of the business model. To implement MRP II, top management must formalize each element of the top management planning process to manage and run the business.

One of the important results of the top management planning process is the agreed upon monthly production plan for each product line or product family. This document becomes an important input to the next major section of the MRP II business model, operations management planning.

OPERATIONS MANAGEMENT PLANNING

BILLS OF MATERIAL	MASTER SCHEDULING	Products
INVENTORY STATUS	MATERIALS PLANNING	Material
ROUTINGS	CAPACITY PLANNING	Capacity

Figure 1-4: Operations Management Planning

Positioned in the center of the MRP II business model, operations management planning develops the detail planning for both materials and capacity. These detail plans are created using management planning as defined in the master production schedule and database information. This information would include inventory status, bills of material and routings.

Master Production Schedule

The *master production schedule,* or MPS, describes the sequencing of the items to be produced. Where the production plan is a monthly plan by product line or family, the master production schedule is normally stated in weekly terms and depicts detail items and quantity of each to be produced. The MPS represents both scheduled customer orders and potential customer requirements. This potential customer requirement acts as an "available to promise" planning sets of material and capacity in advance. Changing customer requirements are managed in the MPS. This is accomplished by reviewing the future status of material and capacity available to support changing needs.

Materials Plan

The MPS is the management input into materials planning. The *material requirements plan* (MRP) defines the detailed material required to support the master schedule. MRP utilizes information from the master schedule, the database of *bills of material* (which defines the specific structure of how the product is made), and the on-hand and on-order status of material inventory so that detailed material requirements can be determined.

From the computer perspective the MRP process can be thought of as a mathematical equation. If "A" is the master schedule or what we plan to produce, multiply this quantity times "B," the bill of material required to produce the product, then subtract "C," the inventory status of what is on-hand and on-order, to give us "D," requirements or what we need. Other item information such as lead time and order quantity provide the time phasing of materials and the amount to order from either the supplier or production.

$$A \times B - C = D$$

| MPS | BOM | INV | MRP OUTPUT |

Figure 1-5: The MRP Equation

Based upon this equation it can be seen that Material Requirements Planning (MRP) is only as good as the quality of the planning process represented through the master schedule and the quality of the data, bills of material and inventory accuracy. Therefore, for MRP to work effectively it is critical for the integrity of the data, bills of material and inventory to be accurate.

Capacity Plan

Capacity Requirements Planning (CRP) is similar to the Material Requirements Planning (MRP) process. Where the MRP process determines the detailed material requirements, CRP determines the capacity requirements. The *capacity plan* is derived from taking the manufacturing information from the Material Requirements Planning (MRP) process and data resident in the routing file. The routing file contains the detailed manufacturing operations process information. This detailed capacity requirements plan projects into the future the load (typically expressed in hours) by work center, department or line in the time frame required to support the master production schedule. These projected load hours can then be compared against current capacity for over or under capacity utilization.

Database Information

The accuracy of the detail material and capacity planning depends on the quality of the planning inputs and the accuracy of the information in the data files' bills of material, inventory and routings. The MPS must state a doable production schedule. The bills of material must define precisely the correct amount of material and be structured in line with the manufacturing process. Inventory quantities on hand and on order must be precise as well. MRP depends on the integrity of each. For CRP, routings must accurately describe the manufacturing process and the time required for each defined process step.

The objective then in successful MRP II implementations is to make accuracy of the bills of material, inventory status and routings a non-issue. The data is accurate — so accurate that no one questions the integrity of the computer data.

OPERATIONS MANAGEMENT EXECUTION

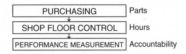

Figure 1-6: Operations Management Execution

The execution phase of MRP II usually is divided into materials purchased from outside suppliers and shop floor production. In the execution of the plan the time frame is at least daily and in many business environments performance to plan and execution is managed in hourly terms. For example, hourly deliveries from suppliers with hourly production and deliveries to customers is common practice.

Purchasing
The output from the MRP system provides the detailed purchased material requirements in support of the master schedule. In essence, the objective will be to schedule the outside shop (our suppliers). Working with the information from MRP, purchasing can begin to communicate and work with the supply base to ensure timely delivery of precisely the right materials at precisely the right time. In today's business environment high performance companies have begun to work with their supply base to make them an extension of their own facility. Oftentimes this results in cross-functional teams between the supplier and the customer working on continuous improvement in areas such as on-time delivery, quality, elimination of incoming inspection of materials, more frequent deliveries, and materials delivered to point of use with the result being supplier certification.

Shop Floor Control
Just as MRP provides the information to schedule the supply base, the detailed material requirements information is available to schedule the shop by machine work center or line to support the master schedule.

Besides providing a daily or hourly schedule to the factory floor, much of the improvement effort in the production area centers around employee involvement. This takes place through utilization of tools and techniques embodied in the principles of Just-In-Time (JIT) and Total Quality (TQ), which results in a habit of ongoing or continuous improvement. These efforts typically take the form of factory simplification to streamline the production process for improved throughput or a reduction in cycle time through production. The improvement efforts then focus on the inhibitors to flow improvement. These obstacles typically take the form of reducing setup time, improving quality, eliminating machine breakdown, improving factory layout, reducing material handling, and cross training for all workers.

Performance Measurement
Financial performance has been the primary measure of success in manufacturing companies. Manufacturing companies have developed financial planning systems and financial statements for measuring their performance on a regular monthly, quarterly and annual basis.

Manufacturing companies have not, however, done as well developing effective operating systems and operating performance measurements to effectively manage business operations and meet business and financial objectives.

Measurement is a very important part of the management process. Setting objectives, developing action plans, allocating resources, assigning responsibilities, implementing plans, and measuring performance for feedback and corrective action are all part of closing the loop on the management process. A definitive set of operating performance measurements helps manufacturing management truly manage the company and its operating performance.

CLOSING THE LOOP

From the business plan to shop floor control, the overall focus of the MRP II business model is to plan and execute to support market-place needs. Delivery to customer need is a bottom line measure of business operations and performance. Delivery, defined by the customer and met on a daily or hourly basis, is the result of the MRP II process.

Closing the loop on the business model, the top management planning process is in monthly time frames, the operations management planning in weekly time frames and the execution phase of the model as previously mentioned is daily or hourly. Therefore, one of the characteristics of an MRP II process being in place is that the plans from the top of the organization are tied together and translated into execution at the factory floor. Over the years we have referred to this as a one plan process. This differentiation is important because in most companies the plans in each area exist but do not necessarily tie together. This might be thought of as disconnects between these plans and functions.

For example, in many companies a business plan may exist but it may be far different from the sales plan in volume and also may be different from the production plan. The production plan may be developed independently of the sales plan because the sales plan is not measured for accuracy and realism. Purchasing could have their own plan (probably tied to ordering material based upon past history). The shop schedule may not reflect the production plan or the master production schedule because of material availability. In this example, which of these is the right plan and how can people be held accountable? The result of achieving the one plan process is that all plans integrate and support one another. High levels of operating performance in MRP II are not achieved apart from a "one plan" process.

CLASS A MRP II

If a company is contemplating the challenge of implementing MRP II, the management team's objective should be Class A MRP II.

CLASS	PERFORMANCE	CHARACTERISTICS
A	**95%**	Complete Closed Loop System. Top management uses the formal system to run the business. All elements average 95% to 100%.
B	**80%**	Formal system in place but all elements are not working effectively. Top management approves but does not participate. Elements average 80-95%.
C	**70%**	MRP is order launching rather than planning priorities. Formal and informal system elements are not tied together. Some sub-systems not in place. Elements average 70% to 80%.
D	**50%**	Formal system not working or not in place. Poor data integrity. Little management involvement, little user confidence in system. Elements are 50% or below.

Figure 1-7: MRP Performance Rating Chart

Simply stated, performance at a level of Class A means that all functional areas in the business model have achieved at least 95% performance on an ongoing basis. In other words, the education and discipline are in place at all levels in the organization to perform predictably at planned levels. It also means that a facility can begin to better understand its potential and abandon conventional wisdom. Let us share a true story with you.

A quality assurance manager was looking at sourcing for automotive valves. The manager looked at two possible suppliers. One supplier made these valves under license from another supplier. The products were identical. Both firms had quality products to offer.

The first firm seemed confident and was mildly profitable. Their cost of quality was high. Much of the cost stemmed from a high rate of rejected material internal to the operation. They did, however, ship only quality products to their customers.

The second company manufactured an identical product. Upon visiting, the second firm was found to be very profitable, sporting a very low cost of quality, with process controls in place in almost every aspect of the factory.

Before leaving each factory, each was asked what their biggest problems were. The answers were interesting. The first firm's response was that they had few problems. They just needed some tweaking to reduce their cost. They seemed very sure of themselves. The second firm, which seemed to have their act together, had a totally different response. Their reaction was one bordering on an adrenaline rush. They said they had so many problems they could wallpaper an office with the list.

The second firm had a better understanding of what areas of opportunity were available. MRP II Class A is a lot like that. Achieving Class A simply means that the company has achieved a high level of predictable or reliable performance. We could say that the business processes are under control, that you have harnessed your business and are controlling the improvements. It does not mean you are done, only that a habit of ongoing improvement has been established in the business. Whenever we hear someone say their firm has "made it," we are immediately skeptical.

Most Class A companies will tell you the same thing — becoming Class A is anticlimactic. If you truly are an "A" company, you realize that it is only the beginning. Although an important one, it is just another celebration point in the process of continuous improvement.

Today, MRP II measurements are reasonably standard and widely accepted, although they vary slightly among educational materials and consulting firms. Using these globally-accepted standards are a good place to start.

The last area we will mention in this overview of MRP II is the people aspects of implementation. It often is an area not given the proper emphasis, but one that can make or break a successful attempt at Class A MRP II.

People will not be set in motion until they are convinced on an emotional level based on trust — until they can say, "That's right! I know that'll make the job easier and improve quality at the same time!" or "It looks kind of hard, but I believe the guy who's telling me this, so it's got to work!" (Shingo, 129)

Shigeo Shingo, Japanese quality improvement guru, makes a good point. People are any company's best and most valuable asset. To successfully see the optimum benefit from any improvement program, accountability and employee ownership in the process must be sincere. Employees generally are keenly aware of change even if it does not directly affect them at the time. There is a constant process of evaluation that goes on in all employees' minds. They are looking for programs and changes that equate to an improved environment for them, higher wages, or improved security. Change that represents a threat to any of those factors will result in employees transitioning into "antibodies" that work hard to disprove any program's effectiveness. We will discuss this very important concept, in more detail, in forthcoming chapters.

COMMUNICATION

For MRP II to work effectively, there must be a process in place that closes the communication loop. The feedback from the sales plan may be critical in understanding the changes in the market. Without this input, the business plan may be simply a pipe dream from the past. On the other hand, maintaining the communication link from the business plan to the sales plan keeps the sales manager designing sales policies and sales incentives that keep the right products in front of the customer. The production plan requires the drum beat of the sales plan to make appropriate decisions around capacities. All of these relationships are critical, from the top of the MRP II structure to the bottom; from the CEO to the dock worker.

Much of the communication needs within a business are actually educational requirements. The mission statement is the first point at which you begin to educate your work force. From that point forward, continuous communication should become your *modus operandi*. We have found that it is impossible to completely communicate and it is nearly impossible to over-communicate. People have developed many habits from many different sources. They look at their job and the world differently. They innocently bring these paradigms to work with them every day. To educate is to empower and to empower is to increase your capacity for improvement. This requires a new kind of management and a commitment to change while at the same time consistency in the method of management style.

Managing in this dynamic environment is not a simple matter nor are the rules iron clad and foolproof. Having everyone educated and informed of the goals of the organization, and empowered at the same time to move creatively within a broad envelope of responsibility, is the goal. Managers must be good listeners and willing to reward risk-taking designed to advance the corporation's mission: a tricky combination, but achievable.

CHAPTER 2

Putting the Business Plan in Place

OVERVIEW

Sun Tzu, a Chinese philosopher and general who lived 2500 years ago, said it best:

> If you know the enemy and know yourself, you
> need not fear the result of a hundred battles. If
> you know yourself but not the enemy for every
> victory gained you will also suffer a defeat. If
> you know neither the enemy or yourself, you
> will succumb in every battle. (Tzu, 2).

Sun Tzu was referring to war with weapon-toting enemies but these ideas seem to fit today's highly competitive markets. It is a battle-field environment and, as Sun Tzu so aptly described, we must know ourselves and our competitors.

The business plan is the responsibility of the president, CEO, GM, or top person in the organization within the four walls of the facility about to implement MRP II. It is the document in which a business describes itself. The business plan presents a vision for the anticipated future, a plan for achieving the vision, a short-term profit expectation, and a definition of the market served. As a business understands its markets, it must understand the competition within that market. The business plan defines the segments of that market and the objectives of the company as it pertains to the market. This document describes the action plan that the entire organization can follow. Lacking such a plan, businesses change directions with the wind, and spend a tremendous amount of energy going in several directions at once.

Of course, the business plan must be designed carefully and accurately. No group of people other than top management can outline the business plan. This plan is the road map for the business philosophy, the reason for the company's existence. MRP II, by outlining the basic structure of a business plan, can only spark some of the questions to ask when putting the plan together. It cannot take the risk out of these business decisions.

THE MISSION STATEMENT

The business plan begins with the *mission statement*, a clear statement of corporate goals that provides focus, such as "to increase our return to shareholders and the quality of our products and services, and to provide a good work environment for our employees." The mission statement provides a management focus.

Today, more and more companies which diversified in the 1970s are realizing that competition is keen and driving them toward specialization. Many of these companies are selling those divisions which do not logically fit their corporate charter and are choosing to focus on one market, following a more targeted mission. It is very difficult to be excellent at everything. The mission statement describes the target areas of excellence. The mission statement is the top level in the business plan hierarchy.

> The whole subject of manufacturing and retailing divides into two classes, not according to size, but according to purpose. If the purpose is to perform the greatest possible service, which in a business way means doing all that is in one's power to manufacture or distribute the

largest possible amount of goods at least possible cost, then the methods will form themselves
quite naturally and according to circumstances.
If, on the other hand, one wants to get the
largest possible profit regardless of service,
then one is not in business and there are no
business rules that apply. It is just a matter of
taking what one can take when one can take it.
(Ford, 250-251)

This quote was made by Henry Ford, the man who put automation
into the assembly process, resulting in an automobile that was
affordable to anyone who wanted one. This was his real mission,
profitably allowing everyone the luxury of automotive transportation. Through this focus he was very successful at this mission by
building all of his cars alike so that his cost was minimized and his
goal met. If his goal was to sell automobiles profitably to those on
the higher end of the economic scale who could afford this luxury,
he would have been competing with other small automobile manufacturers and probably would have built a totally different auto,
focused at competing for those higher end discretionary dollars.

It is the business plan that formalizes this planning process. Mr.
Ford may not have had a formal business plan but he was cognizant
of the need for a business focus. With complex strategies driven by
today's highly competitive environment and employee empowerment allowing more authority to reach the shop floor, writing down
the plan helps communicate corporate intentions and reminds everyone who otherwise might be distracted from the focus.

How many companies can you think of that would gain from shar-
ing their mission and understanding of common goals throughout
their organization? We see company after company with profit leaks
throughout the organization caused by "entrepreneurs" going out on
their own to design what they believe to be the company's focus.
This entrepreneurial spirit is healthy, indeed, but needs to be
employed in the direction that top management has defined. The
objective is not to restrict but to empower; to empower all of the
organization to row the boat in the same direction.

For example, an engineering division within an organization often may be full of independent entrepreneurs. They tend to enjoy certain activities that offer challenging designs and problem solving potential. The danger in leaving this resource unchecked is that these same engineers may tend toward the work they find most satisfying and rewarding. Is this always the same work the customer requires? While it coincidentally may be, it is not always a good fit. We have been involved with companies that have allowed exactly this kind of unchecked effort, resulting in the world's best technology with insufficient market. If we were to point this creativity in the direction of a defined market, spectacular results could occur enhanced greatly by sales.

In today's global market, a company has to wisely chose not only its market position, but also the necessary resources dedicated to maintaining the best position in that market. "Best" is measured not in space-age ideas, but in customer requirements. These top managers must make the business decisions concerning markets served and products offered and communicate them to the rest of the organization. Some leaders have taken this communication to the extent of having the business mission printed on the back of all employees' business cards.

It is important to note that in our studies over the last 15 years approximately 50% of the companies embarking on their Manufacturing Resource Planning journey do not have a business plan. Of the 50% that do, a significant portion have nothing more than a financial plan detailing profit/loss on a monthly basis. A financial plan with financial objectives is an important element of the plan, but by no means constitutes a business plan.

Once the mission statement has been established that defines the vision and values of the business, the management team should define the strategy and tactics to achieve the mission. These strategies and tactics in many companies today are expressed in the form of business imperatives. The business imperatives are the specific actions required to achieve the business mission. For example, one company may develop their business imperatives around the elements of quality, cost, flexibility, reliability, and innovation. Senior management typically agrees on 5-7 business imperatives (with corresponding strategies) to achieve the agreed-upon imperatives.

Also, in each of these elements, specific operating measurables could be established as the management drives to move the organization forward towards achieving the business imperatives. For example, if the business imperative is quality the company could measure parts per million and/or cost of quality as operating measurables. A baseline or starting point would be established and then performance could be measured monthly to gauge progress. Other examples of measurables around the business imperatives could be:

Business Imperative	*Operating Measurable*
Quality	Cost of Quality
Cost	Inventory turns or days' supply
Flexibility	Cycle time or throughput time
Reliability	On time delivery
Innovation	Reduction in time to market for new products

For many companies it is decided that the implementation of Manufacturing Resource Planning (MRP II) could be one of the cornerstones to achieve their business imperatives.

Figure 2-1: Business Planning Hierarchy

FINANCIAL OBJECTIVES

This part of the business plan is less foreign to most organizations. Required by law for tax purposes and required for shareholders to understand their business, the financial plan is the performance measure that keeps the score. Here we find many businesses that are not honest with themselves. It may come from conventional wisdom, intensive training in optimistic thinking, or security through confidence. Whatever the source driver, many businesses, while having this part of the business plan in place, do not optimize its use as a problem solving tool that identifies areas of weakness and forecasts reality. Too many times it is used instead to buy time by forecasting improved profits with no firm plans to substantiate these claims. Eventually it catches up with management when plans are not met, management is changed, or even more frequently, a "reorganization" is executed, which covers up the evidence for a while longer.

In working with one client, they were setting up a financial plan in preparation for a Class A implementation of MRP II. The company had been losing money in this facility for the last four years. Their financial plans for each of these years had shown the proverbial hockey stick, promising to break even in the fourth quarter because of massive improvements that should take place during the year. As we assessed reality, it was obvious that improvements were required, but to what improvement time table could management commit realistically? This facility, which was part of a much larger organization, had a 20% net loss each year. It was simply unrealistic to think that the facility could educate, empower, implement, and execute plans in 12 months that would result in profits.

The financial plan was put together, this time without the hockey stick. For the first time, it showed steady growth in cost reduction through the year and was substantiated with a specific plan to reduce costs in specific areas throughout the facility. The performance curve showed an increase in the rate of improvement. It became exponential, feeding upon itself. In the case of this company, the result was an MRP II financial plan measurement that forecasted a loss for the first year of implementation.

The end to that story is happy, by the way. The second year into the implementation, even prior to hitting Class A, the facility was profitable.

Remember — the goal is twofold: continuous improvement and predictable performance. Once you have achieved these two goals with consistency, you have achieved proficiency and, given a marketable product, your business will survive. (Remember, MRP II does not assure success to a company with no market for its products. The best MRP II implementation possible in a company making wagon wheel spokes will be less than robust.)

The financial plan in many successful businesses centers around the profit and loss statement generated by the financial department. The balance sheet is important as well, but it is mostly of use to top management as they make the tough decisions around the mission and marketplace objectives. The balance sheet normally does not affect the daily decision process as much as the P&L statement. Care should be taken to exclude information from the internal financial measurement that does not reflect actual facility performance, such as investments, leasing portfolios, or other profit aids that are not directly affected by the organization's performance. These still need to be in the measurement for external use (stockholders, IRS, etc.), but should be excluded for internal performance measures. This is not to say that costs of money should be excluded. Capital, if required for the facility, is directly affected by finance costs and should be part of the performance measure.

You might be asking, at this point, if it is possible that two separate and distinct financial plans have to be prepared to meet two separate requirements. Unfortunately, the plans assembled for external use often do not reflect the information needed to correctly evaluate internal performance. We have found that appropriate performance measurements are well worth the time and effort spent on them. They consistently pay back through the adage that "performance measured is performance improved." Failing to create a separate plan when it is needed is not to utilize one of the most important performance measurements in the business. This doesn't mean putting together two sets of books. It does mean implementing measures that help the organization answer the tough "why?" questions.

Most businesses know how to put together an income statement. The *pro forma* for a simple income statement is as follows:

NET SALES	_____
COST OF GOODS SOLD	_____
GROSS PROFITS	_____
EXPENSES	_____
Sales, general & administrative	_____
Net interest expense	_____
EARNINGS PRETAX	_____
TAX	_____
EARNINGS AFTER TAX	_____

Predictable performance along with continuous improvement is the goal.

In addition to the income statement, there are other financial measurements. One worth mentioning is inventory turnover. Inventory is usually a significant investment for a company. In fact, for most companies 50% of the assets on the balance sheet are inventory. When inventory is minimized, it can add to a company's return on investment (ROI). Inventory reduction should be planned as a result of good management practice and not focused on as a goal in itself.

PRODUCT PLANNING

Understanding product life cycles and determining where each of your products fits into the life cycle aids in determining what plan of action is necessary for improved position within the market.

Overall product planning is part of the business plan. The first step is to classify each product according to its stage in the product life cycle. The product life cycle shows stages which all products go through over time. There are four stages, each representing a different stage of development for the product. Each stage may require a different approach to how the product is marketed, inventoried, and manufactured.

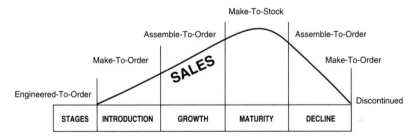

Figure 2-2: Product Life Cycle

Each manufacturing strategy has different requirements and reasons for utilization. As a newly developed product enters the market, uncertainty in demand often requires that customer requirements be generated prior to committing material. Computers were an example in this lower volume, lower demand segment of the product cycle, make-to-order (MTO), a short few decades ago. As the confidence developed in the product, computers became more widely accepted. The market was larger and competition began to require shorter lead times. At that point it was master scheduled at a subassembly level and assembled-to-order (ATO). The product underwent some adjustment in design and application and the machines got much smaller. The resulting product was the personal computer (PC). Demand for these smaller, more efficient machines changed the required mix and, therefore, the manufacturing strategy. Most (not all) companies manufacturing PCs now use a make-to-stock (MTS) process.

All products do not go through all phases of the product life cycle, nor do all products start with the MTO strategy. It depends on customer need, the uniqueness of the products in question, and customer awareness. With the product development cycles shortened to months and technology changing rapidly, the lines between the segments can become blurred. It is very helpful to go through this exercise when determining marketing and production strategies.

OTHER COMPONENTS OF THE BUSINESS PLAN

Each component of the business plan below the mission statement can be subdivided into time elements. The financial statement may go from a five-year strategic view to an annual view to a monthly view in the current year. Product planning also would follow a similar pattern.

Periodic reviews are critical to accuracy. The goal is to be always alert to oncoming declines in market or profitability, a defensive role, as well as being sensitive to coming market changes and adjusting strategy at just the right moment to be one of the first ones (if not the first one) to market, an offensive strategy.

BUSINESS PLANNING CYCLE

Reviewing the Plan

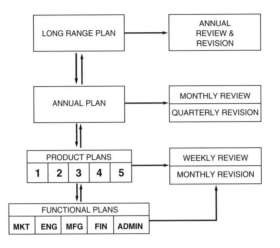

Figure 2-3: Business Planning Cycle

Functional Plans

Each department/division/area within an organization is driven by a plan. These subordinate components of the business plan are driven from directives set from the higher level business plan. These include specific dollar allotments and general product development expectations for engineering, and strategies and dollar allotment for legal liability and/or government interfacing for the legal department. Manufacturing might have certain segments deemed strategic or proprietary. Any such business needs should be spelled out in this, the final segment, of the business plan.

The business plan is the beginning of MRP II. It sets the stage, defines the objectives, and outlines global performance measures integral to the success of every global competitor.

General Tzu:

> When the general is weak and without authori-
> ty; when his orders are not clear and distinct;
> when there are no fixed duties assigned to offi-
> cers and men, and the ranks are formed in a
> slovenly, haphazard manner, the result is utter
> disorganization. (Tzu, 53).

Therein lies the alternative. The world has not really changed so
much in 2500 years, has it?

CHAPTER 3

Sales Planning For MRP II

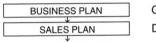

Figure 3-1: From Business Plan to Sales Plan

At this point in the process, the business plan has documented the company objectives and strategy the business will use for positioning product within the market. If the business plan has stated a market share objective, the sales plan must include the strategy to meet that goal and forecast the sales mix based on the anticipated result of the implementation of the sales strategy. This requires a comprehensive knowledge of the market your company serves and the product configurations available from both your company and the competition.

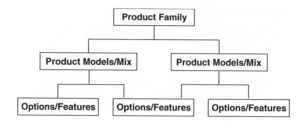

Figure 3-2: Product Family Relationships

A. **Product Family:** This tends to be a broad-based group of products that have common denominators. Many companies complicate this top level grouping by being convinced their products have little or no commonality. Product family misunderstanding is illustrated by a company that explains it has in excess of 100 product families. Generally, if a firm states that it has 100 to 150 product families, it misunderstands the concept of product family. Companies that describe less than 20 families may not necessarily be perfect, but usually are visualizing commonality. While this rule obviously is not foolproof, it is surprisingly accurate. Most companies, after implementing MRP II, have approximately 5-25 product families. It is a bit difficult to document a product family definition that applies to everything from cookies to compressors. Broadly defined, most companies can take global commonality such as shape, or function, or size. Other companies look at less discrete similarities such as the process required, material components, capacity requirements, or cost/price denominators. Look for market application similarities, with the goal of categorizing all products into about 5 to 25 families for top management planning purposes. Automobile manufacturers might divide products into product families such as compact cars, mid-size cars, full size cars, light trucks, trucks, mini-vans, etc.

Product family data are good for calculating capacity requirements and even rough profit estimates. Generally it is not the level at which the sales department should forecast sales, however, except for global budgeting purposes.

It also is important to understand that product line commonality should be a company-wide view. Too often a company's product line is different by functional area of the business. For example, finance may have their own definition of product lines, marketing and sales has another definition (normally market or customer-oriented) and manufacturing has a definition different from both finance and marketing (normally shop capacity-oriented). It is no wonder that in these companies communication and commonality among functional areas is difficult!

In Class A MRP II companies, management has worked together to reach a common definition of product families for use by all company functions. This common product family definition facilitates interdepartmental communication and helps insure a one plan top management planning process. In Chapter 4, "The Production Plan", we also will see the importance of company-wide product families to facilitate the monthly sales and operations planning process.

B. Model/Mix: The model designation denotes differences in characteristics beyond the family. For example, if we use our automobile manufacturer example, model is the designation of Taurus, Civic, Ranger, Explorer, etc. At this level forecasts begin to be useful. The model level has value because it is easier for the sales department to predict sales success accurately at the model level than at the next level — features/options. Companies can (and often do) have numerous models. When assessing your product offering this still should not be confused with optional features that might be available on models. Remember that a Taurus wagon and a Taurus 2-door sedan are in the same model category. The designation exists for planning as well as marketing purposes because of the common components they share. This is often the level at which the trend lines of forecast accuracy potential and planning worth or potential cross.

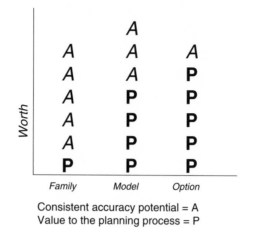

Consistent accuracy potential = A
Value to the planning process = P

Figure 3-3: Example of Worth by Family/Model/Option

The point of this illustration is that the option level offers the most planning value, but accuracy in forecasting is statistically improbable, especially on a consistent basis. At the other end of the spectrum, we find that while family level is much easier to forecast accurately, the planning value is minimal. The middle ground often offers the best answer.

As the people within the sales department become more attuned with the needs of manufacturing through education in MRP II practices, they will develop the forecast process into a more valuable tool — one that manufacturing can use beneficially.

C. **Options/Features:** This designation defines the most detail. At this level we can begin to define the exact configuration the customer has requested or that sales has requested for stock. Using the automotive example, "Taurus, 4-door sedan, blue, with CD player and automatic transmission" would represent this level of detail. You can begin to see how hard it is to forecast accurately at this level. This is not to say that the forecast should not be done for options and features; it must be. The planning process is adjusted when lower forecast accuracy is anticipated but the organization still has to make the business decision as to how much of what it will stock. That decision belongs to the sales department.

INPUTS TO THE SALES PLAN

There are several inputs to the sales plan that must be considered and processed.

- ## History & Experience

- ## Economic Forecasts

- ## Field Sales

- ## Company Marketing Plans

Figure 3-4: Inputs to the Sales Plan

Product history and experience of sales personnel can be of extreme value in developing the sales plan. Most companies review 1-3 years of recent sales history. This provides trends as well as seasonal information for many companies. Very few businesses go back beyond two or three years due to the continued shortening of product life cycles and changing market conditions. Few, if any, businesses can say that what happened ten years ago is a good indicator of future sales.

For many companies economic forecasts or leading economic indicators provide a macro view of what will be happening in the marketplace in the months ahead. For example, in some companies, interest rates may have a particular impact on future sales.

Industries that are affected by movement in interest rates are con-
struction-related products and automobiles. A surge in interest rates
may cause a dip in new housing starts with a corresponding ripple
effect through businesses such as lumber, household appliances and
plumbing supplies.

Field sales input also can be utilized in developing the overall company sales plan or forecast. The more control the company has over
field sales the easier it is to develop a sales forecasting process for
field sales information. In the instances where field sales is under
direct company control the typical process is to have a monthly or
at least quarterly update on future sales. This routinely is by key
account or major customer by territory or region. However, even if
field sales are non-company-owned distributors or manufacturing
representatives it is still possible to survey current and future trends.
In fact, the real trend is for more and more companies to link elec-
tronically with not only field reps and distributors but, most importantly, with the end customer.

When all is said and done — reviewing past history, looking at
leading market indicators, current sales trends, and field sales input
— the company marketing plan must be represented in the sales
plan or forecast. Marketing plans would consist of planned promotional strategy, pricing strategy and product distribution strategy.

Using the aforementioned inputs and data the end result must be a
projection of future sales. The sales department in the
Manufacturing Resource Planning (MRP II) process is responsible
for developing a methodology to deliver to manufacturing an updated forecast of future sales by month in dollars and unit of measure.
This plan or forecast is at least by product line and in most businesses by model mix.

FORECASTING

An important prerequisite to successful production planning is
therefore the forecast provided to manufacturing by sales. In other
words, manufacturing must work closely with sales to develop the
forecast and review it with sales on a consistent basis to help

increase the understanding and resulting accuracy. In the process of developing the plan, a complete understanding of the market is being outlined.

There are two broad-based techniques and components of forecasting: statistical analysis and judgement. Even on the statistical side, the answers often require judgement. It's impossible to be 100% accurate all the time. Well-managed companies understand that forecast variation occurs. The response to the variation comes in two forms. First, after analysis, sales must respond with an updated plan to manufacturing. Secondly, manufacturing must work to improve business execution through process enhancement focusing on shortened lead times and flexibility of manufacturing.

Some sales managers believe that using history to predict the future is a sure fire way to repeat it. There is that danger. The best way to forecast sales is to use a combination of methods. Using history requires a weighted average, giving more importance to recent performance. That alone is not enough, however. If your organization is committed to continuous improvement, then you are initiating new approaches and new products to the market. These new products will affect market performance.

With continued shortening of product life cycles in most companies today, less emphasis can be placed on past history. In today's marketplace looking back even 5 to 10 years gives no indication of future market trends. For many companies the products in the product line did not even exist that long ago.

The forecast should be looked upon as sales' best guess of what will be sold in the marketplace. The forecast is not a plan developed each month with the intent of seeing how far sales can oversell the plan: this most surely will result in the development of a poor production plan. It also results in incorrect stocking of components, unacceptable customer lead times, high cost of sales, and problems with new product launches. This management style actually compromises the company's external reputation by supporting poor delivery performance which results from inaccurate forecasts.

If the sales department is looking for on-time shipments, reasonable lead times, and lowered costs, it holds many of the keys to success. An accurate forecast of product mix allows production to synchronize its capacity with market demand. In fact, working closely with production is paramount in synchronizing the shop and realizing continuous improvement. In many well-managed manufacturing environments, lead times are brought down so tightly that finite capacity planning can be utilized on specific machine centers. This means that the company can use actual firm requirements to commit machine time and component material.

Businesses that utilize a make-to-order (MTO) strategy find that accurate forecasts are just as important as in make-to-stock (MTS) environments. Operations management must be concerned with cost reduction as a driver in its continuous improvement efforts. To be most cost-effective, scheduling of resources — people, training, machinery, space, material, etc. — requires some predictability. Flexibility is a necessity, but is very difficult for any business, even World Class businesses, to react quickly to large spikes in demand with no warning. The sales department, by utilizing the sales forecast, carries the responsibility of providing an early warning system that is as timely and accurate as possible.

FORECAST — BOOKINGS OR SHIPMENTS?

For companies developing and reviewing the sales plan, the forecast is either a shipment plan or a bookings (new orders) plan. In a marketplace that demands quick turnaround of orders where lead times might be expressed as hours and orders ship the same day they are received, there is little or no difference between forecasting shipments or bookings. In this case sales normally represents shipments as the sales forecasted plan. However, in longer lead time environments there may be a big time difference between booking the order and shipping the order. For example, in the aircraft industry the company could receive a customer order requiring a product to be built 12-18 months into the future. In this instance a company could be receiving a higher rate of bookings (new orders) than the present rate of shipments. In this case the company backlog of orders would be growing. Also, the opposite could be occurring, a lower rate of bookings than the rate of shipments. In companies with longer lead times the forecast typically is a bookings forecast from sales and marketing.

THE REVIEW AND UPDATE OF THE SALES PLAN

Soon after the close of each measurement period (in Class A MRP II companies the measurement period is at least monthly), sales and production should convene to review the current performance to plan. Sales has the responsibility in this meeting to reconcile deviations from plan and to revise the forecast accordingly for the next measurement period.

A bookings or forecast review of current sales compared to the forecast is critical. This review by product family and model normally has in attendance sales/marketing, customer service, product managers, master scheduling, materials and manufacturing.

Bookings Review Meeting

Date: MID-MONTH   **Attendees:**

Time: _____

Place: _____

V.P. Marketing/Sales	Master Scheduler
Product Manager	Order Entry Manager
Sales Manager	Customer Service Manager
Materials Manager	Manufacturing Manager

Agenda

    I. Review Past/Current Period Bookings: Forecast Versus Actual

  II. Determine Sales Forecast Revision

 III. Update Sales Forecast

 IV. Publish Minutes

Figure 3-5: Bookings Review Meeting

At the review meeting the forecast is measured in dollars and unit of measure by product family and is totaled. Deviations to plan should be reflected in a revised or updated forecast.

July

| | Dollars | | | Units | | |
FAMILY	PLAN	ACTUAL	%	PLAN	ACTUAL	%
Family 1	$ 17,875	18,550	96	55	53	96
Family 2	100,835	117,900	85	1,505	1,860	76
Family 3	5,820	3,700	64	60	37	62
Family 4	126,00	124,500	99	70	65	93
Family 5	1,350,000	1,443,840	93	45,000	48,128	93
Company Total	1,600,530	1,708,490	93	46,690	50,143	93

Figure 3-6: Sales Plan Performance

In companies aspiring to Class A MRP II levels of performance, Sales is responsible for providing a monthly update to the forecast. The forecast also maintains a 12-month horizon on the plan, so as each month is reviewed the plan is updated. For example, if the forecast plan versus actual is reviewed for the month of July the new forecast would show forecasted sales for August through July or a 12-month rolling horizon on the plan.

Unfortunately there are no Class A MRP II companies (or, for that matter, Just-In-Time or Total Quality companies) that have achieved a perfect forecast. However, some general rules do apply: Class A MRP II companies are achieving 95% accuracy in dollars by product line by month, 90% on the rates of sales or unit of measure by month and by product line, and 85% on the model/mix by month. Whatever the accuracy for the month, the most important thing is the formal review and update by sales and manufacturing. An illustration might be helpful:

In one particular case in a facility several years ago, sales and production were constantly trying to outguess each other. Sales was frustrated at being able to sell more than forecasted, when production couldn't build product fast enough. Production would try to build more than forecast and too often would build what they wanted to rather than what was being sold. It was not a pretty picture.

After they reached Class A MRP II, the sales department felt bad when they oversold the forecast. They didn't feel bad when they sold more: they felt bad that they didn't tell production they were going to sell more.

Feeling this ownership in the overall success drove the forecast toward accuracy. Production began to trust sales. When the forecast was wrong, sales and production, both with a genuine understanding of scheduling requirements, would work out the customer need by reviewing what requirements could be substituted for those more critical They were working together toward a common goal.

CHAPTER 4

Top Management's Handle on the Business: The Production Plan

The traditional position which production has taken over the years has been to second guess the sales department and only halfheartedly entertain the sales forecast. Production would build its own forecast from history and an accumulation of bad experiences. The bad blood between sales and production was so strong at some companies, one might wonder which was the worst enemy, the other department or the competition.

As the discipline of MRP II is introduced into your organization, these old attitudes must be discarded. Trust in the sales department must be fostered. As discussed in Chapter 3, "Sales Planning for MRP II", the monthly review of the forecast by sales and production is critical to eliminate the finger pointing and second guessing. Companies that do not have a monthly review of the forecast along with a monthly update to the sales plan quite often end up with production having an entirely different plan from sales. Again, in Class A MRP II companies there is a one plan process that links all functions in a common game plan. The result of this integrated top management planning process is the production plan — top management's handle on the business.

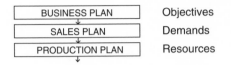

Figure 4-1: The Production Plan

The production plan is developed for each product family. This is accomplished by reviewing the sales plan for the family, together with the desired levels of inventory (for make-to-stock products) or customer backlog (for make-to-order products). Once created, the production plan must be evaluated against the resources required to support the plan. Many factors can be weighed during the development of a production plan. Alternative plans can be constructed for management review and approval. A step-by-step summary of events and a list of information required to develop and revise production plans follows.

PRODUCTION PLANNING PROCESS

1. Calculate production plan rates

2. Review/reconcile with existing production plan

3. Test against resources

4. Adjust/revise production plan; create alternative plans as required

5. Monthly operations review meeting to select the plan

Required information by family

- Updated sales plan

- Target and current inventory/backlog positions

- Planning lead time

- Existing production plan

- MPS summary report

- Demonstrated output rates

- Available resources by month

The production plan supports the sales plan. By taking the information provided by the sales department (the forecast) and inventory or backlog objectives, a production plan can be assembled by product family that can serve as a management's plan for servicing the marketplace.

Production Planning

Determines the production rates and resources required to meet the sales plan and achieve inventory or backlog objectives.

Figure 4-2

The following chart shows an example of a production plan schedule for product family A. A production plan is normally created at the product family level (5-25 families), but information coming from the sales plan in model/mix detail will feed into both the production plan and the master production schedule (MPS). As you look at the chart, be aware that your business decides the proper amount of inventory you need for insurance against variation in the sales forecast and/or unplanned demand spikes. In this diagram, the company has decided to have at least one month's inventory available at all times to guard against stock-out. Your company may operate at a level of discipline that allows much less cushion in finished inventory.

PRODUCT FAMILY A	BEGIN INVENTORY	JAN	FEB	MAR	APR	MAY	JUN	TOTAL
Sales Plan		100	100	125	125	150	200	**800**
Production Plan		125	125	125	175	175	175	
Inventory Plan	100	125	150	150	175	200	200	**200**

1. Production Plan = Sales Plan ± (△ Inventory)   2. Production Rate = $\dfrac{\text{Production Plan}}{\text{Number of Periods}}$

Figure 4-3: Production Plan Make-to-Stock

Notice also that the production plan provides a smooth rate of increase to allow for the most efficient cost of sales on the products produced. The sales plan in this chart is increasing 25% between February and March. This may be perfectly normal in some businesses but would represent a costly capacity jump in others. Each business must administer the production plan as it applies to their particular circumstances, applying the knowledge of the sales department for anticipated customer demand, and the production people for their understanding of the costs of producing the product.

The production plan should have a development and planning cycle similar to that of the sales forecast. With the monthly update of the sales forecast the production planning process should originate and culminate with a new agreed-upon production plan. As with the sales forecast, a monthly review of performance is required to measure variation of actual production to the production plan. Described later in this chapter will be the monthly operations review that, in Class A MRP II companies, ties together the entire top management planning process of business, sales and production plans.

PRODUCTION OR MANUFACTURING STRATEGIES

Based on the customer required lead time, there are different methods of stocking in preparation for firm requirements. Previously illustrated was a make-to-stock (MTS) production plan. This strategy requires units to be in finished goods at the point of a sale. Other strategies also are used. Understanding what your company does and why may help to identify opportunities as you decrease lead time requirements in your facility.

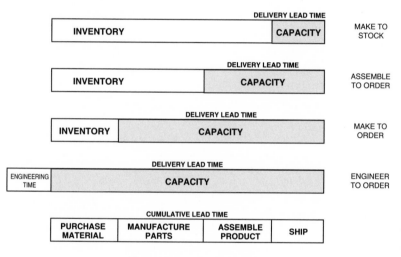

Figure 4-4: Manufacturing Strategy

Engineer-To-Order (ETO)

During the beginning phases of product development, when sales do not support stocking product and documentation is still developing, many production strategists decide to engineer each order as it is received from the customer. An example of an industry with limited demand that has used this strategy for years is shipbuilding. Demand has not reached a point at which stocking components is a requirement. Customers are willing to wait the extended lead time. This is typical of markets with few suppliers. Competition often is the driver behind reduced customer lead time requirements. Another example of an ETO strategy is nuclear power plants. An example more common would be mine drilling rigs which often are designed for the specific project for which the equipment is being purchased. In each of these cases the specific customer requirements call for tailoring the product to the application with normally low volumes of production output.

Make-To-Order (MTO)

The next logical manufacturing strategy along the product life cycle is *make-to-order* (MTO). In this strategy we have a product that has been engineered but does not have adequate demand to justify stocking components. The lead time for MTO is shorter than ETO because the product design already exists. Examples in this strategy include repeat government orders for equipment and even some short lead time requirements such as printing special flyers for a client. An MTO strategy can be cost-effective in the right environment as can each of the manufacturing strategies. The requirements for MTO are responsive capacity, completed engineering, and appropriately matched customer lead time expectations.

Also, as more companies adopt the principles of Just-In-Time (JIT) manufacturing (which results in significant reduced cycle time throughout the business) the MTO strategy is adopted. This is because inventory no longer needs to be positioned to respond to customer orders. The company finds that the improvements in reducing cycle time allow them to make the product after the customer order is received. This improved response or flexibility can be due to factory and business simplification (elimination of cost-added activities) that previously hindered the business operation. Businesses with long cycle times must continue to use either an assemble-to-order (ATO) or make-to-stock (MTS) strategy to support customer demands. This MTO strategy with short cycle times will be illustrated in greater depth in Chapter 9, "Execution of the Plan: Purchasing and Shop Floor Control".

Assemble-To-Order (ATO)

Assemble-to-order is another strategy employed when the customer demand lead time is less than the cumulative manufacturing lead time. This ATO strategy normally is employed by companies when their product does not go together just one way. For example, an electronics manufacturer making switching and graphic systems for use in the audio visual industry might have over a million possible end item configurations. The final configuration is identified by the customer order. Obviously, if the customer wants it in less time than production can build it, something has to be done to prepare for anticipated demand. Printers would stock paper and ink in anticipation of demand; equipment manufacturers would stock components and subassemblies in preparation. This is an especially prevalent strategy used in capital equipment manufacturing because to make-to-stock would require great inventory investments and to build from scratch would not meet customer demand for lead time.

Make-To-Stock (MTS)

Make-to-stock is a familiar strategy in consumer goods such as groceries, drugs, household products, tools, appliances, and cars. When a product is popular enough to require immediate stock at the point of order, the MTS strategy is appropriate.

There are some advantages to MTS that need to be considered and sometimes are overlooked because of inventory level influences. When customer demand is high enough in specific configurations there are advantages to volume production. Costs per unit can be lowered by reducing the setup required and by hard tooling the process (or committing dedicated tooling setup for the specific configuration). There is a trade off here. It can become more cost-effective to "give away" certain options not required to gain volume in another. Automobiles are wired for options that are not always shipped on the vehicles to take advantage of volume wiring harness manufacturing. Automobiles are not offered with specific configurations per customer demand, but instead options are grouped into packages. If the customer wants power steering, power brakes must also be purchased. Pricing is designed to help with the "forced" option choice by making it financially viable. Many businesses that traditionally think of themselves as job shops have not thought through all the possibilities in this regard.

THE PRODUCT CYCLE

Every product has its own life cycle. The speed at which a product moves through the cycle depends greatly on the market it serves. Electronic products have proven that the product cycle can be very short even for higher priced consumer goods. Some companies jump right to the MTS strategy based on anticipated consumer demand. Tee shirts for a political convention would be an example of MTS if the manufacturer were going to sell directly to the convention attendee, the end user. The same tee shirt could be ETO if the manufacturer were building per customer order for a speculative sales distributor.

Understanding and reviewing the strategy for manufacturing is an important part of the production planning process and something that should be done periodically by top management.

MONTHLY OPERATIONS REVIEW

To tie the top management planning process together the Class A MRP II companies have a monthly operations review. The monthly review is conducted the first day (or sometime the first week) of the new month.

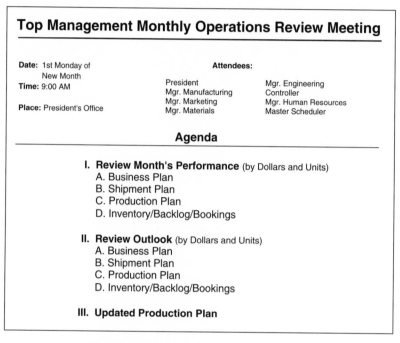

Top Management Monthly Operations Review Meeting

Date: 1st Monday of
New Month

Attendees:

Time: 9:00 AM

Place: President's Office

President
Mgr. Manufacturing
Mgr. Marketing
Mgr. Materials

Mgr. Engineering
Controller
Mgr. Human Resources
Master Scheduler

Agenda

I. **Review Month's Performance** (by Dollars and Units)
   A. Business Plan
   B. Shipment Plan
   C. Production Plan
   D. Inventory/Backlog/Bookings

II. **Review Outlook** (by Dollars and Units)
   A. Business Plan
   B. Shipment Plan
   C. Production Plan
   D. Inventory/Backlog/Bookings

III. **Updated Production Plan**

Figure 4-5: Top Management Monthly Review Meeting

Attendees at the meeting consist of the president and his/her direct reports. The purpose of the meeting is threefold:

1. **Review operating performance from the past month.** This review, by product family in dollars and the unit of measure, measures business plan, shipments, bookings, production, inventory and backlog performance to plan.

2. **Review the outlook for current month and quarter.** Again, the outlook is by product line for the business plan, shipments, bookings, and production plan. Inventory and backlog levels also would be reviewed and compared with target or desired levels of each.

3. **Commitment by the management team to the production plan rates of output for each product family.**

It is important to that note the monthly operations review should not be confused with a company's current financial review. The financial review will look at income and other financial variances where as the monthly operations review is designed to close the loop on the management planning process and make sure all management team members are in agreement with the current direction. (In Appendix A a detailed example of the monthly operations review is presented.)

TOP MANAGEMENT PLANNING SUMMARY

The production plan is the final step in the top management planning process. All three components — the business plan, sales plan, and production plan — require top management's understanding, support, involvement, and commitment.

The business plan is top management's strategic direction for the current year. This plan in many companies typically also goes into the future three to five years. The sales and production plans are senior management's monthly operational plans to drive the organization to achieving the objectives outlined in the business plan.

CHAPTER 5

The Master Production Schedule

The *master production schedule* (MPS) is operations' handle on the business. The business plan may set the course, but the MPS keeps it on track. The master production schedule is one of the key operating plans in a company.

> In achieving control of manufacturing operations, the master production schedule (MPS) is the most difficult and most important set of numbers to be developed. The commonly recognized and probably most important function of the MPS is to drive the formal planning system to initiate procurement of needed materials, work force, money, and other resources. It has many other uses. The MPS provides the best basis for making valid customer delivery promises, for budgeting inventories (direct and indirect labor requirements), for determining purchase commitments, for scheduling engineering and for measuring the performance of manufacturing and marketing groups in meeting their commitments to the basic company operating plans. (Greene, 3.6)

The master schedule must react to customer needs by making decisions within established guidelines, taking into consideration costs to the business, including manufacturing interruptions as well as lost customers. The master schedule is the liaison between sales and production. Many companies make the mistake of treating this schedule with less respect and giving less responsibility to the position of master scheduler than the formal MRP II process requires.

Two organization charts that recognize the importance of the master schedule are represented below:

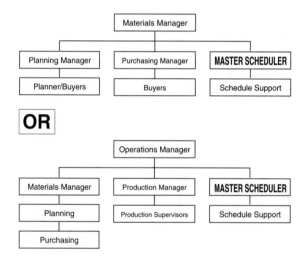

Figure 5-1: The Role of the Master Scheduler

MASTER PRODUCTION SCHEDULE (MPS) COVERAGE

Depending on the business requirements, the MPS can schedule not only MPS assemblies, components, or finished product, but also may drive schedules for engineering, tooling, shift scheduling, purchased material, daily/hourly production schedules and any other resources important to your business. The master schedule truly should be looked at as the master of all other schedules in the business. The limits to the resource linkages that can be made to the

MPS are set only by the limits of your imagination and required resources.

Master Scheduling

Allocates monthly production rates
into weekly production schedules

Based On:
- Product Mix
- Material Availability
- Capacity Availability

Figure 5-2: Master Scheduling Definition

The master production schedule defines the specific mix of products to be produced and the time frame and quantity in which the products will be produced.

FUNCTIONS OF THE MPS PROCESS

- Plan material requirements

- Plan capacity requirements

- Keep priorities valid

- Facilitate order promising

- Contract or plan among all departments

The master production schedule details the model or product mix within the family and is at least updated weekly. It differs from the production plan which is a monthly statement of production by product family.

Each time the master schedule is updated or changed the master scheduler is responsible for reviewing material and capacity to ensure the MPS is realistic. This review of material and capacity normally is done by looking at key materials or long lead time items which go into the product, specifically the items which have lead times longer than the time frame for a proposed scheduled change. This review by the master scheduler is also a rough-cut capacity check of comparing load hours against capabilities by key work centers or areas.

It also should be noted that the master production schedule as shown in weekly time frames is a date-specific schedule. For example, in the MPS for Model 123 the MPS quantity of 11 in Week 1 would be scheduled for a specific day in Week 1.

	ON HAND	WEEK 1	WEEK 2	WEEK 3	WEEK 4	WEEK 5
Forecast		0	12	10	12	10
Demand		10				
Projected Avail. Balance	10	11	10	11	10	11
Available to Promise		11	11	11	11	11
MPS		11	11	11	11	11

Figure 5-3: Product A, Model 123

Forecast
The forecast line of the MPS format is the breakdown of the monthly sales forecast by product family into the weekly detail items scheduled in the MPS. In most business systems software this quantity in the forecast is reduced by entry of actual customer demand.

Actual Demand
The quantity displayed is actual customer demand by date. The date is based upon a scheduled ship date.

Projected Available Balance
The projected available balance is a calculated inventory position which depicts both current and future inventory. The calculation is made as follows:

PAB = (On Hand + MPS) - (Forecast and Actual Demand)

Projected available balance is basically a period by period assessment of supply minus demand. A negative balance on this line indicates that current or future production is less than anticipated demands.

Available to Promise

Available-to-promise (ATP) is the amount of inventory that is available to quote or promise to customer demand in any given period. If in week 2 the actual demand was 8, the ATP would be the MPS 11 minus the actual demand for that week (8), to arrive at an ATP of 3. The forecast in week 2 would also be consumed by the demand (see Figure 5-4).

Master Production Schedule

The statement of scheduled production by time period is illustrated in the MPS line. This typically represents open shop orders in the factory or are planned orders of future production.

	ON HAND	WEEK 1	WEEK 2	WEEK 3	WEEK 4	WEEK 5
Forecast		0	4	10	12	10
Demand		10	8			
Projected Avail. Balance	10	11	10	11	10	11
Available to Promise		11	3	11	11	11
MPS		11	11	11	11	11

Figure 5-4

ATP is simply a tally of product availability scheduled in future time buckets. The ATP is recalculated at each MPS period, and at the completion of a realignment of the MPS. In understanding ATP, it can be confusing since there seems to be no connection between periods. This is true as each period is treated separately. Administer ATP with an assumption that the preceding periods are sold per the forecasted plan. The ATP time phases availability.

Sometimes customers do not want product in the current period. If they specifically request a delivery in the future, the ATP calculation can be very helpful in keeping track of future product availability. The following chart illustrates an example of this type of scheduling of demand.

	ON HAND	WEEK 1	WEEK 2	WEEK 3	WEEK 4	WEEK 5
Forecast		0	5	2	12	10
Demand		3	7	8		
Projected Avail. Balance	10	11	10	11	10	11
Available to Promise		18	4	3	11	11
MPS		11	11	11	11	11

Figure 5-5: Scheduling Demand

Notice the actual customer orders. These are committed from the MPS and are not available to promise and are therefore subtracted from the MPS quantity. There are various ways of calculating the ATP, but all reflect the effect of actual demand on the schedule and treat each period separately.

REALIGNMENT FREQUENCY OF THE MPS

The MPS should be realigned or rescheduled at least every week. Some businesses may find it valuable to do this more frequently. We have found no examples of Class A MRP II companies where the MPS is updated less frequently.

Overly-optimistic companies insist they will "catch up on the schedule" some time down the road. To reschedule is to admit defeat. Such thinking is ludicrous! The MPS should reflect the closest to the absolute truth that your business is capable of predicting. (Remember: You intend to promise customer delivery from the information in your schedule.) If you have manufactured 100 widgets a day for the last 5 weeks and have 125 scheduled, without specific completed tasks designed to increase capacity, there will be little chance that your performance and capacity will increase 25% overnight. Just because the MPS calls for the increase does not make it happen. Capacity changes usually require planned and completed tasks. As the increases are implemented, the MPS can then reflect increased expectations. When schedules are missed, they must be realigned regularly to reflect reality. Customers do not like to be lied to. Running with back orders and missed shipments in the MPS ultimately will lead to inaccurate shipping information being given to your customers, and the creation of informal purchasing and manufacturing schedules. Quite simply because the shop can not believe the MPS they will develop "the real" schedule and suppliers working with purchasing will do likewise.

The MPS realignment is the process of rescheduling the items that are not completed at the end of any scheduling period. This would realign units "past due" as well as units ahead of schedule that have been completed. This can happen if unforeseen circumstances affect the schedule.

The MPS does not have to be smoothed over long periods. If costs associated with capacity change are minimal, the MPS might schedule production much more closely to the forecast than displayed in the chart. Costs included in this decision process are: costs of capacity swings, product carrying costs, shelf life, and customer requirements.

When many items are scheduled, consideration must be given to the give and take capacity requirements of the whole body of requirements. Some units may require X capacity while others may be 2X. Particular unit schedule smoothing may be replaced with overall comprehensive unit schedule smoothing. This process works especially well if requirements normally are not consistent but the process requires a flexible work force trained in several areas to work well. Work cells, or flexible groups of machines and workers dedicated to specific duties, generally support this type of flexibility.

DECIDING WHAT TO MASTER SCHEDULE

Determining what to master schedule relies on the business plan decisions made in the beginning phase of MRP II. Remember that the manufacturing strategy was determined in this phase, i.e., make -to-order (MTO), make-to-stock (MTS), etc. The MPS reflects these decisions.

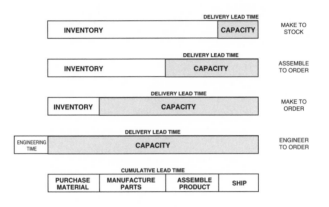

Figure 5-6: Manufacturing Strategy

In an assemble-to-order (ATO) environment a typical company might have a scenario that looks like this:

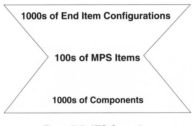

Figure 5-7: ATO Scenario

Let's say that the cumulative lead time is 10 weeks but the customer lead time requirement is normally 4 weeks. In this situation, inventory must be ordered and in some cases brought in to reduce the cumulative lead time to 4 weeks to meet customer demand. This requires inventory to be driven from a forecast. The MPS can do this quite effectively. In this case, sales would help operations develop a model/mix forecast. The materials department might set up phantom bills that would drive requirements but not actually commit material to finished goods. This allows the MPS to focus on a much smaller number than the 1000s of numbers associated with both components and finished configuration possibilities.

PLANNING BILLS

The weekly master schedule translates the monthly production rate into a product mix statement, then breaks it down into weekly production schedules. To break these down into specific items and weekly schedules, the master scheduler must know the product mix by product line.

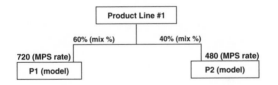

Figure 5-8: Production Plan Rate for 1200 Units

For this example, we will use product line #1 which shows a planned production of 1200. The product mix for Model P1 is 60 percent; for model P2 it is 40 percent. The production rate for each specific model is determined by multiplying the mix percentages by the production rate for the product line.

This means that 720 P1s and 480 P2s should be produced, for a total of 1200. This matches the production plan rate. Once these product mix calculations have been made, the master schedule can be refined further into a weekly or daily schedule. Phantom bills, pseudo bills, or planning bills are different names for basically the same concept. They usually are driven by the MPS. The example above is a simple planning bill.

Planning
Bill Of Material

An artificial grouping of items, in Bill of Material format, used to facilitate Master Scheduling and/or Material Planning.

Figure 5-9: Planning Bill of Material Definition

In most applications planning bills are the essence of the MPS.

THE FINAL ASSEMBLY SCHEDULE (FAS)

Just above the bill hierarchy in a make-to-order (MTO) or assemble-to-order (ATO) environment, the *final assembly schedule* (FAS) informs the final processes of the sequence and quantity of product to be final assembled or completed through the final phases of manufacture. The FAS usually is driven by customer orders and the MPS. It is also a very simple schedule. MRP and the MPS have prepared the business to meet customer demand lead time by having materials arrive in time for the final process. The FAS drives that final process and when each function is done, as agreed to by the schedules, the FAS delivers product to the customer as promised.

The MPS is the marching orders or driver for operations. We cannot emphasize strongly enough how important the MPS is in MRP II. It requires discipline and understanding, measurement, and realignment. The entire organization must understand the discipline and the reasons behind it for the MPS to be most effective. In fact, the minimum level of acceptable MPS performance in Class A companies is 95% performance. In companies serious about customer service and maintaining valid schedules, anytime performance drops below this minimum acceptable level (95%) action plans are developed by operations management to return the MPS performance to within the defined parameters.

EVALUATING THE MASTER PRODUCTION SCHEDULE

Every product has an accumulative lead time associated with either procurement, manufacturing, or combinations of both. There are some natural *time fences* that occur within that lead time. Pictorially they might best be represented by the following diagram:

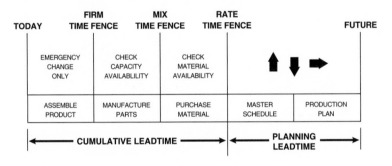

Figure 5-10: Time Fence Policy

Additionally we also might add the customer required lead time which is usually in sync with the firm fence. It is often the reason for the firm fence.

Rate Time Fence

Beyond the rate fence the drum cadence is established. This means the rhythm is established for ordering long lead time materials and planning capacities. This rhythm is important and sets the stage for successful manufacturing schedules. This is as true in JIT environments as in more traditional inventory control practices.

The number of MPS items scheduled in a given period is the rate (or drum beat) and is established in the planning lead time as illustrated above. The forecasted product unit for planning is often at the product family level this far out in the planning window (versus model or specific customer order detail). Outside the rate fence is the planning time, primarily for capacity planning purposes.

Mix Time Fence

In most businesses the mix time fence is the last point on the time line within which to order long lead time materials. It is also the beginning fence for the period required to order model/mix components to be made in time to meet customer lead time demands. This includes items that might be common to a particular model within the product family. In an assemble-to-order (ATO) bicycle business, for example, the mix fence might be the point at which frames must be welded to meet a customer delivery schedule. Specific customer colors and/or options still may be incorporated or committed beyond this stage. Often the mix fence is the level within the product that is master scheduled, allowing the common items to be in process prior to the actual firm customer order.

Firm Time Fence

The firm fence is the one that requires the most discipline. While there are times and circumstances when changes to the MPS will be required, it should be agreed upon by management. The firm fence can be determined at the point at which the production process has met the threshold of remaining lead time minimum requirements to produce products with finished level options and features. In an ATO environment this often is approximately the same period as the customer's lead time demand but it does not have to be. At the firm fence, capacity and material are committed and generally the final assembly schedule (FAS) is in place and progressing. Accepting the firm fence is important for all levels within the organization. Violating the firm fence has costs associated with it and must be part of the decision process each time a violation is considered. On the other side of the equation, to think that the firm fence cannot be violated is naive. When customer requirement situations arise that are not within your control, the sales department and the production department must agree to a resolution. This normally would include deciding which orders will be rescheduled out in place of the orders brought in on the schedule. Production and sales may jointly decide to change the product mix in the master schedule. These requirements must be respected. There are as many possibilities as ideas that the two groups can come up with. The key can reside with the sales department shuffling the schedule just as often as requiring the production group to jump through costly and sometimes impossible hoops.

MANAGEMENT'S COMMITMENT TO THE SCHEDULE

The MPS as well as the FAS are the battle plans that allow the production areas to work at peak efficiency. Management must understand the importance of adhering to the schedule or revising it to reflect realistic changes. We have seen many companies where managers or supervisors will interrupt the schedule to maximize machine efficiencies, allowing (for the sake of cost reduction) parts to be made that are not needed at the present time. While in certain circumstances this may seem appropriate, it works for only a short while and only in machine centers or functions where there is too much capacity — which is a problem in itself.

The only sure way to maintain control over your lead times and schedules is to have an accurate MPS, with changes being made only within realistic reaction time. Once again, do not lie to yourself or, more importantly, don't lie to your customers. Keep the MPS accurate and realign it at least weekly.

CHAPTER 6

Material Requirements Planning

In 1975, when Joe Orlicky wrote the book *Material Requirements Planning*, there was a revolution going on in inventory control. In his book he states:

> The commercial availability of computers in the mid-1950s ushered in a new era of business information processing, with a profound impact of the new technology on the conduct of operations. Nowhere has this impact probably been greater, at least potentially, than in the area of manufacturing logistics, i.e., inventory management and production planning. Until the advent of the computer, these functions constituted a chronic, truly intractable problem for the management of virtually every plant engaged in the manufacture of discrete items passing through multiple stages of conversion from raw material to product. (Orlicky, 3)

He could only imagine at that time what the future might bring. Computers have changed the world, indeed. In the years following his book, most businesses have moved to computer controlled inventory planning. It's interesting that today we are moving from what was total computer control only a few years ago to a simpler means of control, utilizing the computer for the complicated calculations, and realizing that some things are better left in the hands of humans. Just-In-Time (JIT) inventory control has taught the applications and benefits of demand pull systems.

MRP has appropriately evolved as well since 1965. Material requirements planning started out as simply automation of order policy and inventory control. From this original concept, master production scheduling (MPS) and the final assembly schedule (FAS) were spun off, and MRP evolved into an even more powerful tool and an important component of MRP II.

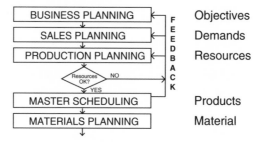

Figure 6-1: The Place of Material Requirements Planning

We all know now that less inventory is good. The American Production and Inventory Control Society (APICS) has certified the fact in publication after publication. Inventory consumes cash, costs 20-30% in carrying charges, requires handling, and takes up space. For that reason, material requirements planning (MRP) has been honed through the years, taking into consideration all available business improvement practices with the objective of just enough inventory. It is a more sophisticated variant of its original form. The basic principles, however (exploding and netting requirements), have not changed.

Material Requirements Planning

Is a time phased priority planning system to schedule material to meet requirements.

Figure 6-2: Material Requirement Planning Definition

HOW MRP WORKS

MRP gets its top level communication from the master production schedule (MPS).

The configurations set in the MPS are passed to MRP. MRP then explodes the bills of material, nets inventory to determine the requirements for each item, and schedules them accordingly. It is a simple process utilizing computers and is nearly impossible to do manually because of the sheer volume of numbers and required schedules at most companies.

The material requirements planning (MRP) process has its foundation in the independent and dependent demand principle pioneered by Dr. Orlicky. The process is quite simple — the only place uncertainty exists in terms of requirements is at the independent demand level. As shown in the following graphic, at the top level in the bill of material —

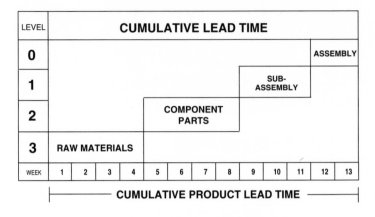

Figure 6-3: Time Phased Planning

— Level 0 or assembly level is the level of independent demand. The remaining levels 1-3 in the bill of material are dependent demand. That is to say, the requirements for levels 1-3 in the bill of material can be calculated and offset for lead time once the requirements at the top level are known. Let's define some terms and then look at an example.

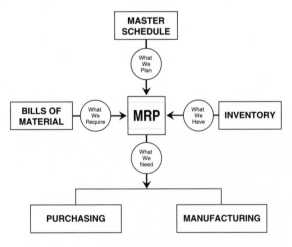

Figure 6-4: MRP Overview

The MPS defines what we plan to produce. In our sample company performance to the MPS is 90%. The bill of material defines how we produce the product. In our sample company bill of material accuracy is also 90%. The inventory status is what material is on hand and on order. Again in our sample company inventory accuracy has been identified at 90%. From this we can determine the detailed requirements for purchased and manufactured material. With MPS performance of 90%, bill of material accuracy of 90%, and inventory accuracy of 90%, the quality of the information from the MRP system being sent to the planners for purchased and manufactured items is 72% (90% x 90% x 90%). Obviously this level of input into the material requirements plan (MRP) is unsatisfactory. The minimum levels of performance for Class A MRP II are MPS at 95%, bills of material at 99% and inventory at 95%.

SOME MRP TERMS

Gross Requirements
Gross requirements are the quantity or demand of an item. This demand may have multiple sources. These multiple sources of demand for the item could come from independent demand, i.e., service parts and customer orders or dependent demand from several higher level items that use the item in common. These gross requirements for the item are combined and summarized by planning period.

Open Orders
Open orders represent an order quantity that has been released to manufacturing or the supplier. If the item is either manufactured or purchased it is considered in process at the vendor and displayed by order due date. It also should be noted that in the case of a manufactured open order, the lower level materials have been relieved from the lower level item on hand balance.

Projected on Hand
Projected on hand presents a running balance of gross requirements minus open orders. Under this method a negative on-hand represents a net requirement. When a net requirement situation exists one

or two actions are recommended by MRP. The first is to search in future periods for other existing open orders that could be rescheduled to cover the requirement. If no open orders can be rescheduled the recommended action will be in the form of a new planned order.

Planned Material Due
Planned material due represents a recommended planned order to cover a negative projected on-hand balance (net requirement). One of the advantages of an MRP system relates to planned orders. Planned orders are replanned or aligned at each MRP replanning session to reset orders with net requirements. Open orders on the other hand are not realigned, but the material planner is given an action message to reset orders with net requirements.

Planned Material Start
Planned material start is the date of order release for a purchased or manufactured item. It is determined by offsetting the material lead time. The planned material start also generates the requirements for lower level items based on the bill of material.

A		ON HAND	1	2	3	4	5
Master Schedule			20		30		30
B ORDER QTY 20 LEADTIME 2			EXPLODE BOM				
Gross Requirements			20		30		30
Open Orders					20		
Projected On Hand		20	0	0	-10	-10	-40
Planned Material - Due					20		20
Planned Material - Start			20		20		
C ORDER QTY 40 LEADTIME 3							
Gross Requirements			60		70		30
Open Orders			40			40	
Projected On Hand		50	30	30	-40	0	-30
Planned Material - Due							40
Planned Material - Start				40			

BOM: A → C1, B1; B1 → C2, D1

Figure 6-5: MRP Logic

In this example the negative projected on-hand for part B in periods 3 and 5 necessitates planned material due in periods 3 and 5 with the start date offset by the lead time. For part C gross requirements are determined by taking the requirements for the master schedule (part A) by time period and adding the planned material starts of part B times the quantity used to build the product by time period. In period 1 the gross requirements for master schedule part A are 20 with a planned materials start of 20 Bs times a quantity per of 2 equals a requirement of 40 Cs from the planned material start of 20 Bs. The requirements on C then in the first period are 20 from A and 40 from B for a total of 60.

With so many calculations, transactions and changes going on, it is apparent that accurate and timely information is very important. The computer software does make the planner's life easier, but good material planning depends on skilled, knowledgeable people who understand the MRP process.

Some products may require thousands of parts and assemblies. Supplier delivery dates may be missed or a critical machine may break down. These types of problems can be the cause of the schedule not being met. If they occur, the planner must take action and get handshake agreements from the people who are affected.

Material requirements planning is the tool which provides the information and calculations, but it is the people who do the work and take action.

Responsibilities

Planned orders are calculated and controlled by the computer system. Material requirements planning recommends to the material planner when it is time to convert a planned order into a purchase order or manufacturing order: however, the physical action must be made by the material planner. It is recommended that all items be coded to a material planner.

Released orders are controlled and maintained by the material planner. The computer system assists the planner by recommending changes to released orders based on the prescribed calculations of

MRP. Again, the material planner analyzes the recommendation and takes what he/she feels is the correct action.

ORDER POLICY

Order policy (the rules of inventory ordering practices) also dictates the cost-effectiveness of the MRP system. Examples of common order policies, in addition to straight EOQ, include: lot for lot, fixed period quantity, fixed quantity, and part period balancing. The global policies which help determine lot sizing and order quantity are critical and should be made by "the business," not left to individual planners. This means management must be cognizant of both the benefits and the downside of each order policy and the ultimate effect on part categories if applied. Order policy should be discussed and debated to determine the best approach for your business. Trade offs include cost, customer service level, and inventory. There is no "right" answer that works in every business every time.

There are few reasons to buy or manufacture more parts than required and we do not want to mislead anyone, but it is wise not to eliminate any approaches to order policy simply because someone said (or you read somewhere) that a particular approach is bad. A total cost calculation is the only sure way to understand the impact of order policy, and it is an important part of setting up the initial policy decisions. Many companies also find that, while they adjust their processes and educate their work force, different order policies result in least cost depending on the manufacturing process in place. If the plant is not yet totally realigned into a process flow, it may be more cost effective to order ten cent items in larger quantities. This same plant, as it reorganizes into cells and more demand pull may then change the order policy for these same items to fixed period quantity, for example, one day's or one week's worth. The point we make is to look at the whole picture. Determine what is best for the existing situation, put plans in place to move forward with improvements, and keep order policy current with the methods your organization is using to manufacture product. Class A companies review order policy at least every six months to ensure least total cost.

ABC ANALYSIS

One tool in helping determine candidates for MRP or JIT is the *ABC analysis*. This procedure applies importance factors to items in the planning process.

Factors affecting the importance of an item and that may be criteria for classifying items in an ABC analysis include the following:

1. Annual dollar volume of the transactions for an item

2. Unit cost

3. Scarcity of material used in producing an item

4. Availability of resources, manpower, and facilities to produce an item

5. Lead time

6. Storage requirements for an item

7. Pilferage risks, shelf life, and other critical attributes

8. Cost of a stock-out

9. Engineering design volatility

(Fogarty, 171)

By using an ABC analysis to stratify the items used for manufacturing, a company can apply different order policies to each level. "A" items usually represent 10-20% of the company's item numbers and 70-80% of the dollar value. "A" items will get the most attention in MRP or, more appropriately, may be assigned a JIT pull requirement order technique. "B" items quite often are established at a 40% quantity, 20% dollar value cut off. "C" items make up the remaining approximately 40% of the item numbers and usually represent less than 10% of the dollar value. Dollar values are determined from unit cost times usage.

Many companies have even chosen to use a "D" category for those items that are small in value, such as hardware or fasteners. This is a change from just a few years ago when companies used to expense these items. There are two schools of thought on this "D" category.

In the 1950s most companies expensed these inexpensive components to monthly operating costs. (This was in an environment of little competition where cost plus margin equalled selling price.) In the 1960s inventory was not yet fully recognized for its costs. Many companies started moving these inexpensive items into inventory accounts to capitalize the value rather than take the operating expense to the profit and loss statement. Today we see companies seeking least cost, moving back to order policies of buying smaller quantities of these "D" items. At some point it again becomes smarter to either empower the shop floor to order its own items or empower the supplier to keep the company stocked.

MRP AND JIT

There is much confusion around JIT and its association with MRP. There is plenty of opportunity for both processes to work together to optimize the performance of your organization.

MRP is a push system, meaning that using batch sizing rules including EOQ and order policy, orders are "pushed" out to the shop floor, driven by both firm and forecasted requirements. JIT, on the other hand, is most often thought of as a "pull" system. Pull systems do not call for product unless there is a firm requirement and do not actually schedule until need is determined. An example is at Harley-Davidson. Lights are activated by the assemblers as they require additional components. Sub-level assemblers build only at the request of the upper level assembler and keep only a small amount of inventory at their station.

> Harley-Davidson Motor Co., Inc. of Milwaukee
> have named their JIT/TQC program M.A.N., or
> Materials-As-Needed. Under M.A.N., Harley

has reduced in-process and in-transit inventory
at their York, Pennsylvania, assembly plant by
$20 million. (Grieco, 19)

MRP and JIT can work very effectively as a single stepped process.
Those items that are less expensive or that economically should be
brought in from vendors or manufactured in larger batches are perfect candidates for the push system, MRP. As the bill structure and
process get closer to final product, there are advantages to using the
pull system, JIT, for assembling these more expensive and valuable
levels. JIT becomes part of MRP II, utilizing both MRP and JIT
techniques.

SUMMARY

There has been opportunity for a tremendous amount of trial and
error since the first installation of a Material Requirements Planning
(MRP) system at the J.I. Case Company tractor plant in Racine,
Wisconsin, in 1961. It is also interesting to note that their installation team required six man years of programming to develop their
system (Orlicky, 119). Today, MRP systems can be purchased for
PC based hardware and turned on in the time it takes to load data
and educate the work force.

It is important to understand that for material requirements planning
(MRP) to be effective it is dependent on the management planning
process and the accuracy of the data in the bill of material and
inventory databases.

CHAPTER 7

Data Accuracy

Decisions are made every minute of every day in a company. Accurate data is necessary to support the decision-making process. Most of these decisions are supported by data that many employees have a hand in creating or capturing. This makes record accuracy very important and extremely challenging.

Record accuracy is a matter of education and expectation. It is amazing how many companies shrug off inventory accuracy as an impossibility beyond 90%. These same companies are quite sure of themselves in terms of payroll. How long would the employees stand for 90% accuracy on their paychecks? When you go to the bank, you expect them to consistently maintain 100% accuracy on your account. Banks have many people involved in your transaction, they have a relatively low pay scale (two excuses often heard for inventory inaccuracies), yet they are very accurate. It's a matter of expectation. As managers you must create a high expectation for data accuracy if you are to get it.

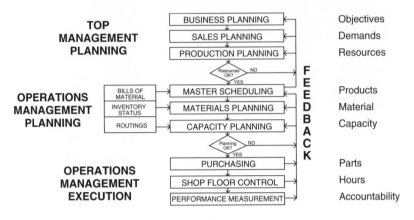

Figure 7-1: Business Excellence

INVENTORY ACCURACY

As discussed in Chapter 6, MRP stock balances are not acceptable at less than 95-98% accuracy.

When it comes to inventory records, the level of accuracy does not pertain to a dollar accuracy based upon a physical inventory. In fact, Class A MRP II companies seldom take physical inventories! Quite simply, dollar accuracy of the inventory is for financial purposes not operational purposes. For example, there are many companies worldwide with 99% dollar accuracy and only 50% inventory accuracy. First, inventory accuracy should be based upon physical count compared to the computer record. A simple example can illustrate this point. In the example comparing the physical count to the computer record if the quantity of the physical count matches the computer record plus or minus a given tolerance level it will be deemed accurate. If the records do not match it will be deemed inaccurate.

Part No.	Count	Inventory Record	Tolerance	HIT	MISS
1	95	100	± 2%		
2	96	100	± 4%		
3	97	100	± 1%		
4	98	100	± 2%		
5	99	100	± 0%		
6	100	100	± 0%		
7	101	100	± 4%		
8	102	100	± 1%		
9	103	100	± 4%		
10	104	100	± 0%		
11	105	100	± 4%		
TOTALS:	**1,100**	**1,100**			

Figure 7-2: Measuring Inventory Accuracy

In the above example there were five accurate records and six inaccurate records. The inventory record accuracy is 45%. In our worldwide studies the norm for inventory accuracy at a piece count by inventory location is 50%!

The only way to keep inventory records accurate is to understand the imperfections in the transaction processing system. Developing control groups and a cycle count methodology are fundamental to determining what is wrong with the transaction processing system in place to maintain inventory records.

Cycle counts and control group counts are process checks to identify the root cause of inaccuracies. In fact, the methodology might be thought of as similar to statistical process control (SPC) techniques practiced for the last 40-50 years.

THE CONTROL GROUP CYCLE COUNT

By taking a sample of high usage items and counting them every day, a company can quickly determine causes for discrepancies. When the problems have occurred within the last 24 hours, transactions are researched easily and errors can be detected. Daily sampling also assists in determining the people involved in contributing to the errors. This allows individuals to receive proper training and the opportunity to correct their mistakes. Sample size can run from 25 to 100 pieces depending on the number of inventory stock locations and the number of people involved in the transactions. If the inventory is not centrally located, as is the case in many facilities today, many small samples may need to be taken.

Each day the transactions associated with incorrect records must be traced to the cause. The objective is not to keep balances accurate by counting them often but instead to eliminate the source (or in many cases, sources) of these inaccuracies. When the control group is consistently accurate (100%), a second control group can be utilized to confirm the measurement.

For most companies, getting to the root cause of the inaccuracy will require an understanding of the transaction processing system. A good place to start to understand the processing system is to create a detailed map of all existing transactions. If the transaction system is like the one in most companies, the system was designed *by* accounting *for* accounting. Obviously, the need in terms of timing of transactions is entirely different for accounting than it is in operations. In operations, the tracking of materials through the manufacturing process are transacted each time materials are moved into stockroom locations. From this view of the transaction system the process can be re-engineered for simplification to meet the needs of operations and 98% record integrity.

Finding errors through "normal" cycle counts is effective as statistically analyzing balance accuracy, but finding the causes often is not as effective and easy using this method alone. Errors detected in cycle counts can be the result of missed or incorrect transactions that happened weeks or even months ago. It is sometimes impossible to pinpoint the error and confront the source of the problem.

CYCLE COUNTING

The five step process for starting a cycle counting program:

1. Measure starting point and post the measurement

2. Education and training

3. Control Group A

4. Control Group B

5. Random/complete/cycle counting (in addition to a mini control group)

There are not many acceptable causes for inaccuracies in inventory balances. In support of good performance measurement activity, cycle counting becomes a necessary evil. Until a company can hold 100% accuracy in balances consistently, there will be a need to cycle count, if for nothing more than to confirm accuracy.

> One immediate issue in the design of cycle counting systems is how to select the items to be counted. The first need is to determine how many items can be counted in some time period (e.g., a day). With a given work force and some estimates of counts per time period per person, the frequency with which each part is counted can be ascertained. Some companies have found it useful to set the frequency of counting using ABC analysis. A items are counted more frequently than B items, etc. (Vollman, 90)

In developing the cycle count program tolerances normally are established in a cost methodology. Using the ABC stratification from Chapter 6, the accuracy tolerances recommended are:

A items = +/- 0%

B items = +/- 3%

C items - +/- 5%

There should be no items with accuracy tolerances greater than 5%.

Class A MRP II companies have found that while cycle counting is still required, it is strictly a performance measurement tool. Where before we might have suggested that all "A" (inventory classification) items be counted at least once a quarter or maybe twice a year, today we suggest that companies do statistical sampling for measurement purposes and supplement with confirmation of zero balances. If everything gets counted when it is at zero, it takes almost no time to count the parts and, if the inventory is turning, most everything will get touched eventually. If any balances reach a negative number, they should by cycle counted at once for obvious reasons.

WHAT CYCLE COUNTERS SHOULD KNOW

1. How and where material is stored

2. Location identification

3. Process to identify items

4. Transaction flow and reporting

5. Cut off controls

6. How to access the on-line system

Cycle counters must be well-versed in the procedures of the warehouse. They also must be able to count! While that may seem too absurd to even mention, such ability is not a given. Many times it is more a result of haphazard attitudes or lack of understanding the importance of the task than it is a lack of mathematical education.

PHYSICAL INVENTORY

Other than cycle counting and control group counts, Class A companies do not perform physical inventory counts for audit purposes. Accuracy should be sufficient to go well beyond the requirements of the financial reporting needs. Accuracy of 95% at the parts per location level using the prescribed tolerance factors will always yield a 99%+ accuracy in dollar value. Measuring accuracy in dollars is a measurement required only once a year for audit purposes and is not recommended as a measurement any other time.

Inventory shrink (the difference between the dollar value of perpetual inventory balances and financial book value of inventory) is nonexistent in Class A companies. Shrink is evidence of lack of control over transactions. In companies where inventory is turned several times per year, shrink should be managed to less than one half of 1% (or .5%). Some common areas in which to look for possible causes of shrink include: reporting accuracy of raw material scrap in assembly operations; reporting accuracy of raw material scrap at primary operations; handling of transactions for inventory shipped out on consignment; inventory transactions for parts shipped out for outside operations; and, although not particularly common, pilferage in some industries (especially consumer goods) can be an issue.

MYTHS ABOUT LOCKED STOCKROOMS

We are not going to say a lot about locking the stockroom, but we are asked about it so often, it seems worth clarifying. The days of mistrust and lack of employee education should be behind us. There may have been a time when business could justify the warehouse fences and inefficiencies of hiding the inventory from the people who needed it, but competition has forced new methods of efficiency. Fences provide only a temporary barrier and challenge to the really determined employee, anyway. Usually the second shift "hero" would learn to scale the fence to get to the required components.

In contrast, today we find companies putting inventory where it is needed, at the point of use. Employees are educated to the benefits of properly recording transactions such as scrap. This is especially important when backflushing is used to capture component usage. (Backflushing is the automatic inventory adjustment transaction for components, based on the completion of the next higher level assembly.) The adage "What's in it for me?" is very appropriate here. When assemblers realize the linkage between accuracy and elimination of shortages, they become much more conscientious.

Shigeo Shingo also has words of wisdom on the topic of people appreciating the need to understand. Shingo:

> Akira Shibata, executive director of Daiho
> Industries, once gave me a good piece of
> advice. Although it is considered important to
> have a good grasp on "know-how," know how is
> not enough by itself. He explained that "if
> know-how is all that is being passed along, you
> won't know what to do when conditions change
> or the least bit of trouble crops up. If, on the
> other hand, you also understand why things are
> the way they are — the "know-why" of the task
> — then you will be able both to cope with
> changes, and to apply your knowledge to other
> tasks. (Shingo, 68)

Logistical fences and gates are expensive testimonials to the fact that the company is either unwilling to train employees, or just doesn't have faith and trust in them.

WHAT ABOUT ELIMINATING THE STOCKROOM?

Many companies are moving in the direction of having no stock-room facility as such. Some even have accomplished the goal. These companies have taken what used to be centrally stored and issued it to the work centers, decentralizing the inventory to point of use. There are many good reasons to position inventory at point of use:

1. Less inventory is required.

2. Material is more accessible to the worker requiring it.

3. Ownership in the accuracy of material is placed with the worker using the material.

4. Higher customer service results.

Point of use storage of materials will require a lot of company education prior to component dispersion. Employees must understand transactions and the effects of those transactions on the part procurement process. This can take some time. We have found that the best way to make this transition is to apply a steady process of displacing the stockroom rather than doing it all at once. By taking segments of assembly support components to "point of use" in a scheduled, planned sequence, education can be enhanced with experience. Wins can be publicized and perpetuate the process.

ROUTING ACCURACY

Routings, the steps and road map to the manufacturing process, also must be accurate. One common situation involving routings is lack of understanding on the part of production personnel — not because they lack knowledge of the correct routings, but because they may not value correct paper work. After all, the job is to produce product. In fact, they may not utilize the process sheet at all. It may be wrong from the point in time when the engineers designed the product or due to engineering changes which have not caught up with daily production (another problem!). Inaccurate routings often are compensated for by production personnel who "know the ropes." These operators will tell you that the routings "don't make any difference if they are right or wrong because nobody looks at them anyway." While this may seem perfectly logical to the production personnel, it is not a good reason to allow inaccuracies to exist.

The routing defines the sequence of operations and production time required to produce the product. In Class A MRP II companies minimum levels of accuracy are 98%, which means 98 out of 100 routings are correct. To measure the accuracy a simple audit can be conducted on several products to determine the types of inaccuracies and if there are problems with the process to develop and maintain routings or the process sheets. If manufacturing audits routings and bills of material for errors, a simple form (Figure 7-3) that can travel with the work order through the process steps is recommended.

BILL OF MATERIAL AND ROUTING AUDIT FORM
Please note any inaccuracies in the process sheet attached to this audit form and turn the audit form into your supervisor at the end of the shift.

BOM/ROUTING AUDIT

Item No. <u>1234567</u>   Description _____

Shop Order No. _____   Auditor _____

BILL OF MATERIAL REVIEW

	YES	NO
Complies with specifications?		
Specification complies with process?		
Notes comply with specification?		
Required correction		

ROUTING REVIEW

	YES	NO
Complies with specifications?		
Specification complies with process?		
Notes comply with specification?		
Required correction		

ECN REQUIRED

YES ☐   NO ☐   ECN NO. _____

If Yes forward to Documentation

CORRECTIONS	FOLLOW UP
Approved by	By
Keyed by	
Comments	

Attach additional information on seaprate sheet if required

Figure 7-3: Bill of Material and Routing Audit form

Inaccuracies are noted and turned into the process owner (typically a manufacturing engineer) for review and correction. Again, in Class A MRP II companies the goal for correction of bills of material or routings is a 24-hour turnaround for fixing errors.

It also is important to point out the impact of Just-In-Time (JIT) practices on routings and their accuracy. In Chapter 9 "Execution Of the Plan", manufacturing work cells will be discussed. As companies adopt JIT principles for waste elimination, factory rearrangement for flow and throughput become major factors. One of the methods employed to improve throughput can be manufacturing cells. Manufacturing cells typically are for a product family set up for flow by rearranging and dedicating equipment. The implications for routings and their accuracy are obvious. The process is simplified in that the product is produced through dedicated equipment and standard processes which ultimately may lead to the elimination of the need for routings altogether.

BILLS OF MATERIAL

Bills of material are the basis through which MRP creates material requirements. Additionally, bills of material are utilized by numerous functions throughout the business enterprise:

> *Engineering* — the product structure is developed and maintained by engineering in most companies.

> *Planning* — the bill of material is utilized to plan, schedule and order material.

> *Production* — utilizes the bill of material to manufacture and define parts for production.

> *Accounting* — the bill of material is utilized to cost the product.

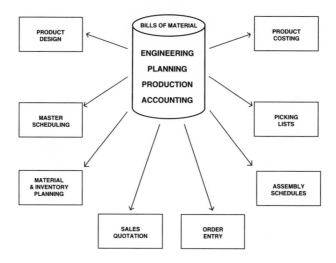

Figure 7-4: Bill of Material Uses

Both inventory levels and shortages can be affected by the accuracy of bills. Many companies find that as they focus on bill accuracy, components that are used in numerous places are not called out in all of the configurations. Assemblers, especially those who have been on the job for a while, usually do not look at the bill documentation. If they look at anything it is usually the drawing — which is part of the reason why the drawings may be more accurate than the bills in a lot of companies.

Another common problem is finding parts called out on drawings that are not synchronized with routings and processes. When this happens, parts can be delivered to an operation and not used until some subsequent operation, These loose components infrequently make it to the point of use correctly. These too are candidates for correction.

As many companies begin their MRP implementation, they find there is more than one bill of material system in place. In fact, some companies have 3-4 bills of material systems. For example, engineering might have a bill of material system as the original designer of the product, and this bill of material might currently reside in their computer system. Manufacturing may have an altogether different bill for the same product. This could result from improvements or changes being made in manufacturing without feedback to engineering. Also, materials could be utilizing a bill of material for ordering material that is different from both production and engineering. This happens all the time in companies with poor engineering change processes. In addition, accounting could be working with a bill of material for product costing that also might not be the current product structure. Obviously, the answer in Class A MRP II companies is that they have one bill of material system that everyone (all functions) utilizes.

*The Bills Of Material define the product to
meet the needs of all functions of the company*

The Bill of Material System Is A Company System

Figure 7-5: Bill of Material System

Bill accuracy is the heart of material requirements planning. Bills of material drive the ordering and scheduling of components. They determine how many and when they will be ordered. The planners have to rely on the information provided in these bills, for without it they would have to second guess everything and, in effect, would not even be able to get the benefits of using a computer to net requirements. It is surprising how many companies do not understand the significance of accurate bill structures. Bill of material accuracy is not acceptable at levels less than 99%, a higher level of expectation than for any other data base element.

In achieving 99% accuracy of bills of material many of the principles discussed in routing accuracy also apply here. First, the process owner typically is engineering or the function/person that originates the product structure. The process to measure could be accomplished by using the bill of material and routing audit form previously described. Again, errors should be corrected in 24 hours.

When measuring bill of material accuracy the elements measured should be at least part number, quantity per, description, and proper structure. These are the elements that MRP looks at in the planning process. Accuracy then would be defined as the number of bills of material accurate as compared to the total number of bills of material measured. To achieve 99% accuracy, 99 out of 100 bills of material measured would be perfect. This measurement may sound harsh, but think of the accuracy requirements in pharmaceutical manufacturers! Inaccuracies found could be analyzed using tools similar in achieving inventory record accuracy.

ENGINEERING CHANGE

One of the important aspects of maintaining an accurate bill of material is managing engineering change. As a product is improved or revised over time, it is essential that the bill of material be maintained in a timely manner to reflect the correct component materials consistently. Because every department uses the bill of material records to perform their daily tasks, accuracy and timeliness is critical.

Changes in a product can alter features offered to customers, impact materials procurement, or result in changes to costs and profitability. Failure to manage the engineering change process effectively can result in significant cost-added activities within the organization.

Being effective in the engineering change process requires that all users of the bill of material be involved. This involvement typically is documented in an engineering change procedure. The procedure outlines the steps to be performed which result in an updated set of engineering documentation, including the bill of material and engineering drawings.

The procedure also defines the steps to communicate the change to all functional areas within the business.

Engineering change can be either planned or unplanned. Periodic, planned improvements to products can be managed and scheduled to ensure a smooth transition to new suppliers, materials, components, or production processes. Unplanned change is all too common, and the mishandling of coordination of these changes adds significant cost to the business.

Whether planned or unplanned, each engineering change must be managed. A step in the engineering change procedure is to determine the timing of the change. Some changes may be enacted immediately. Although the cost of component material or product obsolescence can be high, the effect of the existing product in the customer's hands may be higher. The majority of engineering changes are enacted at a date positioned in the future. Using an effectivity date, Materials can coordinate the transition within the materials plan, Production can coordinate change in production processes and inventory can be managed to reduce the obsolescence which arises from the change.

The technique of applying effectivity dates to the bill of material records acts to plan the consumption of materials under the old product configuration while at the same time planning the future materials to support the new configuration. Material requirements planning supports the appropriate materials plan to correspond to the effectivity dates stated in the bill of material.

The bill of material becomes an archive of the changes to the product configuration. Date effectivity can be accessed to determine customer service information and assist service and repair operations.

While determining the effective date of an engineering change can be based on a variety of management inputs, the management of the change is a planning activity. This coordination is normally the responsibility of the master scheduler.

Data accuracy is a prerequisite to the successful use of material requirements planning (MRP) and achieving Class A Manufacturing Resource Planning (MRP II). For instance, the engineering change process might be identified as a root cause of bill of material inaccuracies. The first step would be to make a detailed map of the current process. From the mapping, non-value added activities or redundancies could be identified and eliminated, achieving a process simplified and streamlined for throughput.

CHAPTER 8

Capacity Planning

The initial capacity planning phase of the business is the responsibility of top management and takes place during the development of the production plan as described in previous chapters. This top management planning of capacity deals with the broad base resources required to support the long range needs of the business. It is high level in nature, and does not get into the detail required to manage capacity for each machine center or other detail resources.

In this chapter, the final step of operations planning, comes the detail plan required to understand the bottleneck threats or barriers to success in executing the manufacturing plan.

> Capacity requirements and available capacity should be expressed in the same terms for purposes of comparison.

> Measures such as pounds, gallons, feet and pieces provide for straightforward comparison of required and available capacity. Measuring required capacity in standard work hours, a method used in many organizations, involves multiplying the product volume by standard time requirements for each operation.

> In many situations there are certain facilities
> whose capacity historically has been greater
> than required capacity, and examination of
> future requirements is only necessary when
> substantial changes in volume occur. There are
> also bottlenecks: work centers where available
> capacity often has been inadequate or barely
> adequate. It makes sense to determine the
> required capacity for these work centers first,
> since they are the most likely constraints on
> output. (Forgarty, 17-18)

High performance companies spend their time wisely, concentrating on only bottleneck work centers. Planning the capacity in detail in other work centers, especially ones with excess capacity, is not a value-added activity. In most companies there are fewer than half a dozen critical work stations. Like the orifice in an hour glass, the restriction is not throughout the process, but at a single point. Bottleneck work stations act in this manner. High performance companies manage these bottleneck areas in the master production schedule. Using this management process a capable schedule can be created rather than schedules being dictated by a machine center's inability to produce to market demand.

Identifying the bottlenecks normally is not a problem in most companies: there are usually several people in the organization who can name the bottleneck work centers off the top of their heads. A good guess at who might know this information is the assembly manager and/or the shop supervisor responsible for daily build schedules. They deal with the restrictions in these problem areas daily. Having identified the work centers to focus on, there are at least four opportunities that follow:

1. **Adjust the bottleneck to allow production to correspond with the market demand for the product.** This often can be done by alternative shifts, adding manpower, reducing equipment changeover times, procuring more equipment, increasing efficiency, subcontracting, etc. This is a good alternative and with the proper planning, flexibility can be planned into the

processes with cross training and duplicate tooling, allowing resources to be shifted depending on shifts in market demand.

2. **Provide alternative processes that allow for parallel paths at the bottleneck operation,** in effect increasing capacity using other means. Many companies ignore this option because alternative methods often are less efficient than the normally scheduled process.

3. **Change the process to eliminate the bottleneck as a necessary resource for production.** This option takes some creativity and imagination, but often is the best answer. One of the best sources for such alternative ideas is the work force in the bottleneck area. It is difficult to suggest generic ideas in this book that would scan the entire industrial base, but there are numerous examples of success out there. Examples include: forming parts to eliminate welding smaller components; using locking fasteners rather than screws and bolts which can take longer to install; combining more than one operation, for example, combining deburring and machining operations; eliminating extra handling, etc.

4. **Adjust the master schedule to synchronize with the restriction.** This is okay as long as there is no incremental market opportunity available that is being passed up. If this is the only option, when it is exercised, information should be passed back to the production plan at the top management level so that appropriate action can be taken to increase capacity if the market will continue to support it. It is rare that it pays to refuse to service a market opportunity and it always seems a shame to pass up sales. Sometimes it is the only answer to truthfully schedule product delivery.

When calculating the requirements on bottleneck work centers, take into consideration all the factors that limit capacity.

Demonstrated capacity is the level at which the operation has been performing, not what we wish it could do consistently. Keep standards for capacity planning accurate, that is, match them to actual experience. When actual performance exceeds standards, and output capability has increased, adjust the standards to reflect the improvement. History must be examined and factors changed to remove the bottlenecks.

SETUP REDUCTION AS A MEANS TO INCREASED CAPACITY

Setup is defined as the time which elapses between completion of the final piece of a production run and the first good piece of the next production run. Setup is very seldom a value-added exercise. Eliminating or reducing it can only aid in an effort to increase capacity. Many manufacturing processes can yield upwards of 30% additional capacity just by eliminating wasteful setup operations. There are two categories of setup:

1. **Internal Setup:** The time that is required in a nonproductive mode, to change an operation from producing one item to producing another item. On a machine tool, it is the time that it takes to change the fixture or machine settings that must be done with the machine shut off and not producing parts up to the time of the first good piece or product on the new job.

2. **External Setup:** Pre-work that is done while the operation is still producing items in preparation for a change from one item to another item. In the machine tool example, this is work done off the machine to aid in quick conversion. This can be done by the machine operator or other designated resource. The machine can and should continue to produce while external setup is being done.

It is to the benefit of the business that internal setup be limited to what is absolutely necessary. This becomes especially important in bottleneck work centers where additional productive time is desired.

Reducing setup time reduces the economic order quantity (EOQ), which reduces work in process inventory.

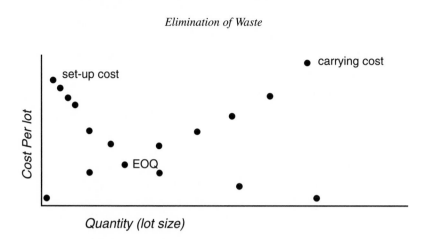

Figure 8-1: Economic Order Quality (EOQ)

From the diagram it can be seen that as setup times are reduced, EOQ is reduced proportionately. Setup reduction is key to reducing the costly effects of bottleneck work centers in the business.

Setup time can be reduced in almost every case. Work force education followed by directed involvement of the people in the work center requiring set up improvement often results in reductions of more than 50%.

ELIMINATION OF WASTE

The last area in this section to adjust capacity is the elimination of waste.

Dr. Shigeo Shingo, in his work in the Toyota production system, determined seven types of waste:

1. **Waste from over-production.** This is probably the worst kind of waste. Over-production results in inventory being made that is not required and ties up money that could be used to improve the business. This resource could also be reassigned to make inventory in response to demand.

2. **Waste of waiting.** What could be more wasteful than having required resources waiting for components or tooling, etc?

3. **Transportation waste.** Material handling is a part of lead time that adds no value. Lead time length is proportional to the amount of inventory required. The less material handling the business requires, the less inventory required.

4. **Processing waste.** Processes that require decision making and human intervention by nature create some waste. "Fool proof" fixturing helps eliminate this. Also steps in the process that might at sometime in the future be eliminated could be considered processing waste.

5. **Inventory waste.** Any time the business creates inventory that is not required, exposure to obsolescence, spoilage, shrinkage, pilferage, etc., is heightened. Although inventory is listed on the asset side of the balance sheet, it is a liability until it is sold.

6. **Waste of motion.** Any amount of time, motion or effort could be a non-value added activity. An example of wasted motion could be taking material out of one container to put into another container.

7. **Waste from product defects**. Defects are a multiple sin since they are examples of wasted time, material, energy, and money. There can be no conscionable excuse for this impiety! (Suzaki, 12-13)

DETAILED CAPACITY PLANNING

In developing the detailed capacity plan there are many similarities with the materials plan. Detailed capacity planning is developing a scheduling and loading system that plans capacity to meet the requirements of the master schedule. The capacity planning process accesses the information in the routing file (work centers, setup, run and queue times) along with the planned and released orders from the material requirements planning system. Each manufacturing order is back scheduled using the routing or process sheet. The back scheduling is by operation with each order receiving start and due dates. This determines the time frame the load will hit the work center.

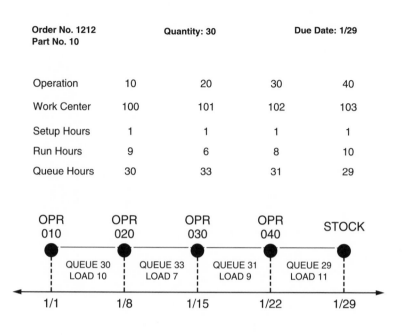

Order No. 1212 Part No. 10	Quantity: 30		Due Date: 1/29
Operation	10	20	30	40
Work Center	100	101	102	103
Setup Hours	1	1	1	1
Run Hours	9	6	8	10
Queue Hours	30	33	31	29

Figure 8-2: Load Scheduling

All manufacturing orders are summarized into a load profile. By work center and time frame, the load profile shows the hours required to support the master schedule. This capacity plan is available as often as the material requirements plan is generated. For example, if the materials plan is generated weekly each supervisor would receive a detailed capacity plan for his/her work center showing load hours each week.

Work Center	Package	Past Due	1	2	3	4	Total
LOAD	Released	100	500	400	300	200	1500
	Planned		100	250	350	300	1000
	Total	100	600	650	650	500	2500
	Capacity		500	500	500	500	2000
ANALYSIS	Variance	-100	-100	-150	-150	0	-500
	Cumulative	-100	-200	-350	-500	-500	80%

Figure 8-3: Load vs. Capacity

In most business systems the load hours or load summary is displayed in either bar graph or numerical format. The hours of load by work center show as far into the future as projected by the master schedule. If, for example the master schedule goes out 12 months into the future, the supervisor for the work area can see a detailed load profile that far into the future. The ability to review capacity beyond backlog or hard orders is one of the key resulting capabilities of a material requirements planning and capacity requirements planning process.

PLANNING LEVEL	PLANNING FUNCTION	LENGTH OF PLAN HORIZON
Top Management Planning	Production Plan	Long Range 1-5 Years
Operations Management Planning	MPS MRP CRP	Medium Range 1 - 3 - 6 Months
Operations Management Execution	Shop Floor Control	Short Range Weeks Days

Figure 8-4: Capacity Planning Levels

The capacity planning process can be looked at on three different levels: The production plan looks at capacity issues nine to twelve months or longer into the future, the master schedule or master production schedule (MPS) and the detailed capacity plan most generally focus on one, three and six months into the future, and at the shop floor level the daily schedule of capacity needs for the current week and following week can be analyzed.

CHAPTER 9

Execution of the Plan: Purchasing and Shop Floor Control

PURCHASING

Most companies purchase a significant portion of their material for manufacture. On average at least 50% of the cost of the product is purchased components and raw material — for some, such as electronics manufacturing, purchased material might be 70-80% of the cost. In today's competitive environment companies find that it is nearly impossible to be excellent in every function, and companies that specialize often can provide the product and service most cost-effectively. Gone are the days when businesses strove to be completely vertically integrated. High performance businesses focus on their core competence.

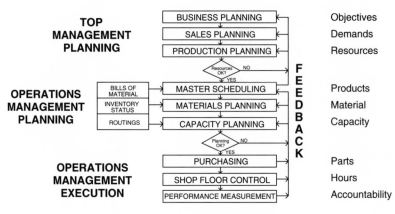

Figure 9-1: The Business Excellence Model

This move toward more dependency on suppliers requires improved relations. They must be treated as an extension of the operation.

Called partnerships, these relationships no longer include bluffing and withholding facts to seek lower prices or playing multiple suppliers against one another. Instead suppliers should be chosen carefully and with long-term commitments in mind.

Question:

What Does "SUPPLIER PARTNERSHIP" Mean

Answer:

A total management commitment to a cooperative supplier relationship provides the lowest total costs by allowing the focus to be applied to the important non-price areas of cost.

Figure 9-2: Supplier Partnership Definition

SUPPLIER PARTNERSHIPS

Class A MRP II operations are quick to share knowledge, information and improvements if it can help the supplier do a better, more cost-effective and defect-free job providing product. The list of elements of a supplier relationship is:

- A long-term commitment

- Cost-based price negotiations

- Shared quality assurance goals

- Frequent and open communications on schedules, problems, and solutions

- Multi-disciplined organizational inputs and communication, not just buyers talking to sales people

- Teamwork and cooperation by and with both parties

- Technical assistance to suppliers

Let's look at the elements that make up the supplier partnership.

Long-Term Commitment

Long-term commitment does not mean moving next week from supplier A to supplier B because "we can get a better price". Long-term means establishing a relationship that is mutually beneficial to both parties (win-win). This effort typically starts with key suppliers with shared goals around quality, lead time improvement, on-time delivery and material fit for use or packaged to be delivered to point of use on the factory floor.

Cost-Based Price Negotiations

The focus should be on total cost — not price. In our studies approximately 40% of the total cost of a purchased item is non-price. These non-price areas could include incoming inspection of material, rework of material, de-trashing or disposing of incoming packaging material, material storage, cost of purchase orders, and material movement. The focus should be on the elimination of these non-value added activities.

Shared Quality Assurance Goals

Quality in this case should be looked at as the "big Q" of Quality rather than just the "small q" or quality of the material. Shared goals as previously mentioned could be in the areas of lead time reduction, improved on-time performance, reduction in lot or batch sizes of incoming material, elimination of incoming inspection and improved quality of the material. These goals and the progress towards the goals could be reviewed monthly.

Frequent Open Communications

Open communications and multi-disciplined organizational inputs in today's business environment are important. As companies try to eliminate non-value added steps from their processes the number of brokers who move information or handle material subsequently are being greatly reduced. Producers are talking directly to their internal and external customers. In supplier partnerships this means the hourly people producing the product in one factory are in direct communication with the hourly people using the product. The advantage is that producers get to understand the customers' precise needs.

Technical Assistance to Buyers

Assistance can be in many forms, from providing education and training to the supply base on improvement principles such as statistical quality control, problem solving, setup reduction or manufacturing resource planning (MRP II) principles. The general principle is to share knowledge and improvements made in our own processes with our supply base.

GETTING STARTED WITH SUPPLIER PARTNERSHIPS

Once the concepts of supplier partnerships are embraced the question becomes of "how and where to start". Figure 9-3 depicts one company's starting point with the continuous improvement process in the supply base.

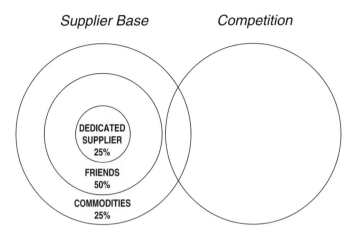

Figure 9-3: Purchasing JIT

Most companies start with dedicated suppliers. In other words, those with whom they have had a long-term relationship. Start with 5-10 suppliers of strategic importance to pilot the concept of supplier partnering, then expand beyond this group to a second tier, and finally to those commodities purchased from suppliers who also may be doing business with the competition. In this group, the commodity area supplying the competition, obvious care should be given to how and what improvements should be shared.

There are at least two outgrowths from the supplier partnership: (1) development of a supplier certification initiative where previously defined shared goals exist, with a reviewed habit of ongoing improvements and, (2) a reduced supplier base.

Experience has shown that as a company begins to look at the supplier base and how many suppliers there are for a particular part, product or service it becomes painfully clear that working with all of them is not realistic. In fact, their criteria for current existence (which one will give us the best price?) will not be the future criteria for evaluation.

As supplier relationships are developed it is logical to begin to think of the supplier base as an extension of our own shop or factory. This now means one of the goals should be to communicate the master schedule or materials plan to the supplier.

Supplier: ACE Equipment

PART NUMBER	JANUARY				FEBRUARY				MARCH
	8	15	22	29	8	15	22	29	
A					5		10	15	40
B						10		10	25
C			10	15	20	20	20	15	85
D		5	10	15	10	15	10	10	50
TOTAL	**0**	**5**	**20**	**30**	**35**	**45**	**40**	**50**	**200**

Figure 9-4: Purchasing Schedule Release

In the example shown the output of the materials plan has been given to the supplier to plan materials and capacity. In today's business environment this schedule can be conveyed through electronic data interchange (EDI) from the manufacturer's scheduling system to the supplier's system. This eliminates the need for purchase orders and their associated costs. The schedule provided to the supplier may go out numerous weeks into the future, but not all of the schedule would be considered firm. For example, in automotive and appliance industries the release or schedule may show the next 12 weeks but not all of that horizon is firm by mix and rate. The information shown could be viewed as having the supplier deliver on a weekly basis (deliver supply parts/materials on Friday for Monday production). There are numerous companies where this information is broken into not just weekly requirements but daily or hourly.

When achieving daily or hourly deliveries with the supplier, the signals for actual production material required could be conveyed through pull systems. The more frequent the delivery the closer those using the material need to be with those making the material. Closer does not necessarily mean physical distance, but applies to previously discussed shared goals, frequent open communication and multi-disciplined inputs.

108

SHOP FLOOR CONTROL

In Class A Manufacturing Resource Planning (MRP II) companies
one of the most noticeable characteristics is the transparency of the
schedule, from the top of the organization to the factory floor.

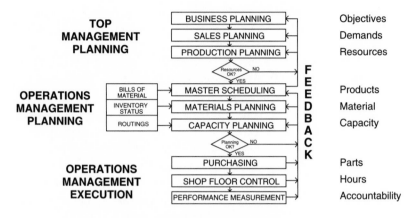

Figure 9-5: Business Excellence Model

There are no disconnects. In other words, what was developed in
the monthly production plan (rates of production by product line)
has been converted into the weekly master schedule (model/mix)
and now into a daily schedule or priority list. Most importantly the
Class A MRP II companies run to or execute the schedule.

DATE 6-30-X

WORK CENTER	PART NO	ORDER NO	OPER NO	QUANTITY			SCHEDULE		
				ORDER	COMPLETE	BAL.	HOURS	START	DUE
102	*5202	12333	010	10	0	10	5	6-27-X	6-27-X
	5210	12444	020	25	0	25	5	6-30-X	6-30-X
	*5201	12345	020	100	50	50	50	7-01-X	7-07-X

* AVAILABLE AT WORK CENTER

Figure 9-6: Work Center Priority Dispatch List

The validity of the daily schedule (sometimes referred to as a dispatch list or priority schedule) is one of the true tests in a business as to how well the MRP system is working in the company.

A simple illustration might be helpful. Suppose we went to the factory floor and asked the supervisor if we could see the daily schedule and the response is "Do you mean that thing that comes out of the computer area?" The supervisor ultimately finds the daily schedule with today's date on it and we ask if the job on the top of the list is the job being worked on. The response is, "No, we have no material for that job." We then ask if the second job is the one being worked on and the response is again no, as there is a quality problem. Our third question is the same as the first two, "Is the third job on the list the one you are working on?" Again, the answer is no. This time the reason is because the tooling is broken. The final question then is what job on the list is being worked on? The answer from the supervisor is that the job being worked on is not on the list! The true schedule is derived from a shortage meeting held each morning. The schedule is a handwritten list kept in the back pocket of the supervisor. How well was the MRP system working? Obviously not very well in the shop! The flip side of this example would be a Class A MRP II company where the job at the top of the schedule is the job being worked on. There is consistency from the production plan through the master schedule to the factory floor.

To keep its schedules in sync, the Class A company typically has a daily 15-minute stand-up meeting with MRP planners/schedulers and shop floor supervisors. The stand-up meeting is to review the daily schedule. The talk centers on the activities required to hit schedule: materials, capacity, quality, etc. If the schedule is going to be missed the discussion includes a plan to reschedule and get back on schedule.

JUST-IN-TIME PRODUCTION

In a competitive business environment time becomes a most important resource. Part of Just-In-Time production involves reducing manufacturing cycle time or creating a "responsive production environment." This responsiveness to change in customer demand or changes in marketplace conditions are precisely the key objectives of Just-In-Time production. In today's traditional factories there are a number of items which inhibit Just-In-Time production. The focus on specialization with specialized equipment results in a functional manufacturing facility. A *functional layout* or functional manufacturing is where like machines are grouped together to form a work center or department. For example, lathes are grouped with lathes and drills are grouped with drills.

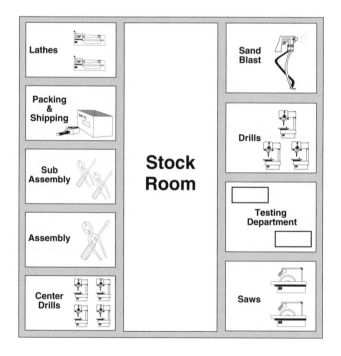

Figure 9-7: Functional Manufacturing Layout

Manufacturing products or materials are moved from one machine to another based on the routing for that product. A product may move back and forth across the manufacturing floor several times before it is completed. When work arrives at a work center, it waits in queue until all preceding work is completed. Then work begins on the order and continues until all of the material or pieces are completed. At that point all of the pieces are moved as a group or batch to the next work center. This process is completed at each individual work center until the product is completed. This means that the time to produce a product in a functional manufacturing environment is usually long. In the functional layout the focus is not on the efficient flow of materials but the efficiency of each individual operation at each work center. With the movement of material back and forth across and throughout the factory several times during the product process we might begin to call this type of manufacturing, "scenic manufacturing." This manufacturing layout is characterized by long manufacturing cycle times, high ratios of motion to work, more cost-added than value-added activities going on in the factory, and worker and machine specialization.

With functional manufacturing, production is typically batched in larger lot sizes. Many parts have multiple levels in the bills of material which necessitate a large number of individual manufacturing orders to build the product from raw material to a finished item. With many manufacturing orders in process on the floor at the same time, a high volume of computer transactions is required to track progress and report status. This often leads to:

- Long lead times in manufacturing
- Poor visibility of problems
- Delayed problem resolution
- Inefficient use of floor space
- Large quantities of work in process

FROM FUNCTIONAL TO STRUCTURED MANUFACTURING: THE EXAMPLE OF VALVE MANUFACTURER A

Valve Manufacturer A, located in Rockford, Illinois, is a good example of a functional manufacturing process utilizing Just-In-Time production techniques. The valve manufacturer typically manufactured their products in lot sizes of 500.

Step 1: Lathe operation

Step 2: Mill operation

Step 3: Sand blast

Step 4: Center mill

Step 5: Return to stock

Step 6: Issued back into production for subassembly operations

Step 7: Torque operation

Step 8: Relubricate operation

Step 9: Drill operation

Step 10: Return to stock

Step 11: Issued back into production for final test

Step 12: Final assembly

Step 13: Return to stock

Step 14: Issued to pack and ship

This process can be envisioned in two ways. First, imagine starting the production process at the valve manufacturer with an imaginary ball of twine. Unravel the ball of twine as the product proceeds from one operation to the next, stopping, of course, when the product is returned to stores. At the end of the process measure the length of the unraveled twine which is the distance the product traveled during production. At this company the distance was 4000 feet.

Also, in terms of time, the manufacturing cycle time was measured with a calendar. It took four weeks of elapsed time from raw material until a finished product existed.

The competitive environment for the product at the valve manufacturer was that the product was viewed in the market place as a commodity item. This meant the lead time for the product had to be very short. Customers would wait only days, not weeks, for the product. Therefore, from the company's viewpoint, the manufacturing strategy was to carry finished goods inventory in anticipation of customer orders or make the product to stock. Other important results of the functional layout manufacturing process for the valve manufacturer were two-hour setups on equipment, numerous work orders to manufacturing in process at the same time, labor reporting for each operation, numerous inventory transactions and a 15% reject rate of material during the production process.

Lot Size:	500
Bill of Material:	4 levels
Inventory Transactions:	8
Floor Space Utilized:	4000 feet
Manufacturing Lead Time:	4 weeks
Setups:	2 hours
Labor reporting:	by operation
Work Orders:	Yes
Output:	20,000 per month
Quality:	15% reject rate

Figure 9-8: Valve Manufacturer Functional Layout Summary

Structuring the Flow

In its pilot project for JIT the valve manufacturer intended to physically link all of the valve manufacturing operations. This meant determining which equipment was required to serve the production process. The objective was a layout that provided for continuous flow and minimized the distance between operations. This meant grouping machines in a manufacturing cell often called a C cell or U line layout. A factory within the factory was created.

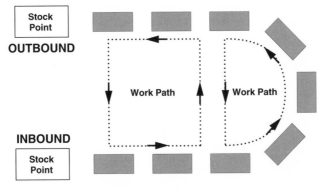

Figure 9-9: U-Line Layout

In structuring the flow in the cell an interdependency between operations was created. There was emphasis on improving the total process rather than the efficiency of each individual operation. Any problem that interrupted the flow of product become more visible and was highlighted. It required immediate resolution. For example, downtime due to machine breakdown or a quality problem stopped the entire process. Each worker was given the responsibility and authority to stop production when problems arose. With the interconnection of all operations this meant a stoppage in the entire work cell. This created a sense of urgency where the problem must be solved in order to keep the revenue (product) stream flowing.

The success in the valve work cell over a 6-month time frame was typical of the results achieved in JIT companies. The cell was able to produce in lot sizes of one rather than batches of 500 or 1000 as was previously the case. In addition to developing continuous flow in a cell, the reduced lot size also resulted in reduced floor space. The distance the product now traveled was down from 4000 feet to 40 feet. This not only provided for a compact plant layout, but also changed the way material was handled. In the functional layout material was moved from work center to work center by lift truck or hand truck. This meant material handlers, usually considered indirect labor, were utilized to move material between operations. In the cellular layout workers at each operation moved material as part of the job. Manufacturing cycle time was reduced from four weeks to one hour. The focus on cycle time reduction had a significant impact on quality.

Previously when quality problems arose, the rejected material was sent to an area of the shop to be reworked. With the manufacturing cycle time being four weeks rejected material normally was scattered through the entire production process. Finding the source of the reject was next to impossible. The new environment of the cell meant that any rejection of material could not have occurred more than one hour ago. This also meant almost instantaneous feedback on quality problems.

This instantaneous feedback carried over to downtime of equipment due to equipment failure or lengthy setups. All of the interruptions were looked at as problems by the workers in the cell. The objective then was to "protect the flow" of material within the cell.

In the functional layout protection of the flow of material or the insurance policy against interruptions is accomplished by carrying work in process inventory to buffer the problems. In the cellular layout or structured flow manufacturing the inventory insurance policy against interruptions must be replaced with higher quality, shortened setups on the equipment and preventative maintenance.

Valve Manufacturer A: Functional vs. Structured Layout

	Functional	*Structured Flow*
Lot Size:	500	1
Bill of material:	4 levels	1 level
Inventory transactions:	8	1
Floor space utilized:	4000 feet	40 feet
Manufacturing lead time:	4 weeks	1 hour
Manufacturing strategy:	Made-to-stock	Make-to-order
Setups:	2 hour	15 minutes
Labor reporting:	By operation	None
Work Orders:	Yes	No
Output:	20,000/month	80,000/month
Quality:	15% reject rate	0.2% reject rate

Other Examples

Not all manufacturing operations lend themselves to cellular layout and dedicated equipment: however, the concepts of structured flow manufacturing and continuous flow still apply. In many businesses there are pieces of equipment that cannot be dedicated to a specific product line, but are used by all product lines in the business. Examples of these types of operations are heat treat, testing, plating and painting.

A hardware manufacturer for doors and windows located in Owatonna, Minnesota, provides a good example of structured flow where equipment cannot be dedicated. For their pilot in JIT they chose a window hinge product. The manufacturing process for the hinge consisted of a stamping operation with the raw material being coiled steel. From the stamping operation the second step was to degrease the hinge. Operation three was to plate the hinge, and operation four was assembly of the hinge. Each of the four operations was located in a different area of the plant. Due to environmental restrictions, it was not feasible to move the equipment closer together or have it dedicated to any one particular product line.

A team was assembled consisting of personnel from each of the functions involved in the hinge manufacturing process. Their objectives were to shorten cycle time, improve response to the customer and improve quality. The team devised a standard container that could be used at each operation. Until the standardization of containers, each operation had its own container which resulted in excess material handling. The standard container was now the signal to start production, meaning that when an area received empty containers, it was the signal to produce more. The standard container also held only 1/50th of the previous lot size. This obviously meant that setups had to be reduced significantly.

It also is important to point out that JIT improvements in the manufacturing operations can and should be applied throughout the entire business. An example is a water well screen manufacturer located in St. Paul, Minnesota. Their improvements in moving from the functional layout to structured flow are listed below.

Well Screen Manufacturer: Functional vs. Structured Layout

Before	After	Improvement
6,000 sq.ft.	2,500 sq.ft.	3,500 sq.ft.
14 people	8 people	6 people
Work-in process 6,000 sq.ft.	Work-in-process 1,600 sq.ft.	Work-in-process 4,400 sq.ft.
325 ft. travel	105 ft. travel	220 ft. travel
Quality problems	Quality visible	Less rework
Rework large quantities	Rework small quantities	Less scrap work
On-time delivery 70%	On-time delivery 99%	Happy customer
No employee input	Major employee input	Ownership at each cell
Work order per line item	Work order on McJohnson form	1,000 pieces of paper
Labor reporting per work order	Labor reporting per monthly work order	Labor reporting now reduced by 15 minutes per person per day Errors also reduced
Material per work order	Kanban	1 man team

Cycle time in the manufacturing area had been reduced to one day. The problem now became one of order entry and engineering. With each product requiring some engineering design work the paper-work flow and office administration had a cycle time of several days. This lengthy flow in administration negated improvements made in the manufacturing process because the customer expected quick turnaround on their order. This caused the company to stock many shapes and sizes of screen. The answer at the water well screen manufacturer was simple: Apply what had been learned in the shop to the office. Cells by product line were created, each cell containing order entry, engineering and production control. Now orders go to the floor in a matter of hours after the order is received from the customer.

Another way to think of structured flow manufacturing is as "expressway manufacturing". Rather than taking the scenic route when the manufacturing process starts, the objective in production is to get on the on ramp when the product is started and to the off ramp when it is completed.

EFFECTIVE STRUCTURED FLOW MANUFACTURING

There are several important components of making manufacturing cells or structured flow manufacturing work effectively. First, it is imperative that workers are cross-trained to perform multiple tasks within the cell or work area. The objective of the cross-training is not to move workers around to keep machines busy, although this certainly was the case in the functional layout. The reason for cross-training is twofold: to move people to prevent an interruption in the flow of material, and to provide a different set of eyes looking at the process. With different people looking at the process ideas and suggestions will tend to increase.

The second component is that new equipment should be purchased for its simplicity. Its ability to be modified and changed over are important features. The objective then is improved flexibility. In the functional layout, equipment was purchased based upon how fast it could run, or how many pieces it could make in an hour. The main drivers for the equipment purchase based upon how fast it could run were efficiency and utilization. There was no consideration given to its flexibility in areas such as time to change over or setup the equipment or maintenance of the equipment.

The third component of structured flow manufacturing is that the process or cell should be balanced to the rate of consumption at subsequent operations. Cell or operation output is not based upon a machine rate or the ability to produce, but is adjusted to the rate of sales. Also, in many cells, output rates are adjusted by adding or subtracting workers.

BENEFITS OF JUST-IN-TIME

1. Elimination of inter-operation inventory.

Products are processed through operations in much smaller quantities. Ideally the process quantity is a lot size of one rather than the larger lot batch sizes traditionally found in the functional layout.

2. Simplification of the process and administration.

Just-In-Time can be thought of as factory simplification. Processes are simplified and interconnected. In a functional layout, where manufacturing cycle times are measured in weeks, conventional tools are utilized to track and control production operations. Manufacturing work orders normally exist with labor reporting by operation, schedules exist for each operation, capacity is planned by operation, and efficiency and utilization are tracked by work center.

In JIT with cycle times reduced, conventional tools to track and control production are not required. Much more of the control is visual. Work orders typically are not required and the need to report labor is no longer appropriate. Reporting mechanisms now are focused on reporting finished product or output per hour or per day against the plan. For those companies utilizing material requirements planning (MRP) systems the significance of moving to JIT is important. The computer systems now must operate in a work orderless mode with minimal reporting. Also, instead of scheduling operations and capacity by work center, there is now only one schedule for the entire cell or work area. Capacity is now developed at the master schedule level rather than at a detailed capacity requirements planning (CRP) level.

3. Elimination of levels in bill of materials and stockroom transactions.

In the functional layout, material typically travels in and out of the stockroom several times before completion of the product. This results in several levels in the bill of material structure and frequent inventory transactions. Again, for companies utilizing MRP-type systems each level represents a different part number with a work order for each level in the structure and an inventory transaction for each time into the stockroom and each time out.

Just-In-Time streamlines the process resulting in flattened bills of material (reduced number of levels), ideally to one level. Material now moves out of the stockroom as raw material and returns as finished product with elapsed cycle times often measured in minutes or hours. For MRP systems, the single level bill of material that reflects the new manufacturing process allows for simplification of MRP with a master schedule and a schedule for raw materials.

4. Quality improvements through immediate feedback.

As a result of reduced cycle times and improved worker communications, problems are discovered and corrected almost immediately. No longer are quality problems being detected that occurred in upstream operations weeks ago. The key variable becomes time. The detection process is simplified because the problems that surface occurred just minutes or hours ago, not weeks.

5. Improved worker alertness through a variety of tasks.

Workers are now cross-trained to have multiple skills. People are rotated into different jobs within the work area so everyone can do every job. This leads to a new set of eyes constantly looking at the process which results in a higher number of suggestions for improvement in the work area. Flexibility and response improves because workers can now move to keep material flowing. Again, structured flow has significant implications for workers and management compared with a functional layout. In the functional layout, workers become specialized. The focus is to become excellent at a particular trade or operation. The result of specialization is the proliferation of labor grades. Again, functional excellence is stressed, with no focus on the total process. With Just-In-Time production labor grades are reduced theoretically to one, with each worker capable of doing any one of the jobs. Because of this, compensation might be structured based upon the number of jobs mastered rather than striving for achieving the highest level within a classification.

6. Worker moves material as part of the task.

Instead of using material handling equipment to move material from one operation to another numerous times (all cost added activities) each worker may perform the task of moving material to subsequent operations.

7. Less supervision.

Workers are cross-trained to perform any one of the tasks and trained in basic problem solving skills. The result is a highly motivated work force solving problems, implementing suggestions for improvement in the work area, interviewing employees to work in the area and training fellow employees. For the supervisor, the traditional role he or she has occupied changes dramatically. Now he or she must become coach, facilitator and teacher.

GETTING STARTED WITH JUST-IN-TIME

Most companies do not have the luxury of getting started with a new factory. Most factory layouts have just evolved, so getting started means rearranging the present facility. Multiple cells or structured flow processes can be created over time.

The most successful JIT companies start their initiative with a pilot. The pilot project consists of selecting a pilot product line or process. It is important to remember that the pilot should be an aggressive undertaking. In other words, do not pick a product line that is being phased out of the business or represents an insignificant amount of revenue contribution to the corporation. Being aggressive means starting with a product line that is one of the company's key revenue generators. Once the pilot has been selected, begin rearrangement for better flow. The less distance the product travels the better. Once the factory rearrangement has transpired establish standards for housekeeping and work place organization. This means allowing time during the day to perform housekeeping duties, and providing a checklist for the workers in the area that defines specifically the tasks to be performed daily. As the cell work area is created it is imperative that people in the work area receive extensive cross-training and are educated in basic problem solving skills. Once production is activated in the area, any interruptions in the flow are irritants. It is, therefore, important that those who work there be able to identify and solve problems as they arise. Companies that have not cross-trained and armed the work force with basic problem-solving skills have found workers in the area ill equipped to solve the vast array of problems they now encounter — and consequently the JIT initiative fails.

With the introduction of the pilot the work area should begin to reduce the lot or transfer batch size. Ideally, this should be done consistently until a lot size of one is being transferred between operations. It has been our experience that each time the lot size is reduced a new set of problems arise. These new problems should be looked upon as opportunities for further improvement in the work area. As the lot size is reduced, the new problems that might be encountered could be material handling, setup time on equipment, line balancing and process cycle time for an operation. Remembering that interruptions in the flow are problems, a preventative maintenance program will be critical to prevent unplanned downtime due to machine breakdown. This will be another area where daily checklists are used for workers to perform routine maintenance on a daily basis. Again, just as we talked about allowing time out during the day for housekeeping and work place organization, routine maintenance should be performed at this time.

The final actions in getting started in the JIT pilot are making extensive use of the work force's new problem-solving skills in the area to solve problems and continuously improve. The pilot should be looked upon as the area for training in JIT for the work force, where new ideas are tried and JIT concepts practiced. Once the new concepts have taken hold in the pilot the next step is to duplicate the process in another work area.

TWELVE ELEMENTS OF JUST-IN-TIME

Based upon our experiences, a company should look at Just-In-Time through three management areas: technology management, people management and systems management. Each area includes four elements of JIT.

Three Key Management Areas In Any Manufacturing Business

- **Technology Management**
  Objective: Responsive Production Environment

- **People Management**
  Objective: Capability For Rapid Improvement

- **Systems Management**
  Objective: Careful Application Of Resources

Figure 9-11: Three Management Areas For Viewing JIT

Technology Management Elements

The elements of technology management are:

- Structured flow manufacturing

- Small lot production

- Setup reduction

- Fitness for use

The objective of the technology management area is a "responsive production environment." This means developing flexibility to respond to changes in individual customer demand or marketplace conditions, or to produce to customer orders of one or a thousand.

Structured flow manufacturing incorporates the concepts of continuous flow manufacturing. The focus is on flow and throughput to reduce the cycle time through manufacturing. As previously referred to, it should be noted that many companies have applied the concepts of structured flow manufacturing to the office environment to shorten cycle time in the total business process. Structured flow manufacturing typically involves factory rearrangement to group technology into manufacturing cells for organized throughput.

Small lot production means producing the product in ever decreasing lot or batch sizes until the theoretical lot size of one is reached. The ability of producing one at a time provides the opportunity to make every item every day. This, in turn, provides the flexibility of responding to customer requirements and meeting those requirements which otherwise could be met only through inventory.

Setup reduction or quick changeover is the process of minimizing equipment downtime between material changeovers. Setup time could be thought of as the time from the last good part of the previous job to the time of the first good part of the new job. The overall objective of reducing setup or changeover time is to facilitate small lot production.

Fitness for use was coined by Dr. J.M. Juran in defining the principles of quality. Fitness for use means understanding and meeting the customer's precise needs. The basic principle is that at each step in the business process there is a customer. Not all customers are external to the business; there are also internal customers. Internal customers could be the next work center in the manufacturing process or design engineering handing off products to manufacturing in which case manufacturing is the customer to design engineering.

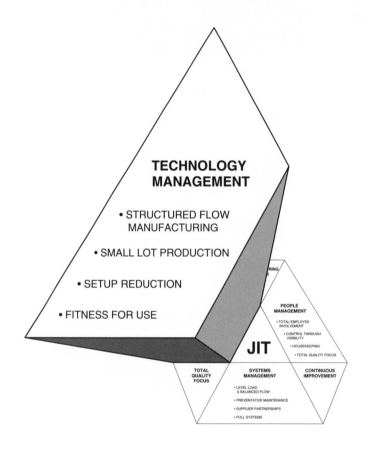

Figure 9-12: Technology Management Elements of JIT

People Management Elements

The people management elements of JIT are:

- Total employee involvement

- Control through visibility

- Housekeeping

- Total Quality focus

The objective of this area is "capability for rapid improvement." This means that improvements transpire in the total business process on an ongoing or continuous basis. Continuous improvement is achieved through involvement of people at all levels in the organization.

Total employee involvement is required to achieve the objective of the people management area of "capability for rapid improvement." Only through everyone's being involved in the improvement process can a company achieve continuous improvement in its processes. Employee involvement and continuous improvement will be achieved through Small Group Improvement Activities (SGIA). SGIA is a structure created to focus on improvements by utilizing employee knowledge in the work area.

Control through visibility provides a visual status of the production environment. The objectives here are to communicate the goals, highlight problems and attack waste. The element of control through visibility is oftentimes looked at as an extension of basic housekeeping, the idea being that as unnecessary items are removed from the work area, it becomes much easier to see and thus work on process problems.

Housekeeping or work place organization means a highly organized and efficient work place. Housekeeping is sometimes thought of as "a place for everything and everything in its place." Organization in the work place will facilitate improvements in other elements such as setup reduction, pull systems and quality. Improvements in housekeeping pave the way for waste elimination by reducing unnecessary movement or motion.

Total Quality focus is fundamental to Just-In-Time production. Total Quality can be defined as striving to continually reduce process variability. Variation in the process, albeit quality problems, lengthy setup times or fitness for use issues, is considered a problem and must be improved continuously to achieve Just-In-Time production. As process variability is reduced, total employee involvement is required to redefine the customer at each point in the process in order to provide products and services that are "fit for use."

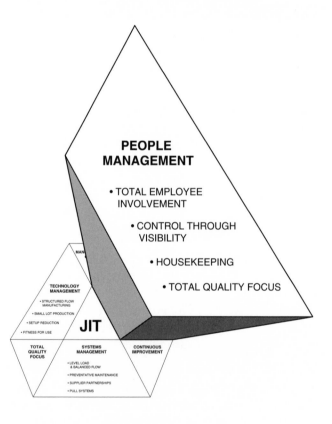

Figure 9-13: People Management Elements of JIT

128

Systems Management Elements

The Systems Management elements of JIT are:

- Level load and balanced flow

- Preventative maintenance

- Supplier partnerships

- Pull systems

The objective of the systems management area is "careful application of resources", which means using all company resources wisely. This can be achieved in Just-In-Time by extending equipment life, eliminating over-production and developing efficient production processes through the use of pull systems.

Level load and balanced flow means organizing production processes for scheduled throughput. Leveling and balance become control mechanisms. The objective, synchronous production, is achieved by repeatability and predictability in process cycles.

Preventative maintenance in Just-In-Time is developing reliable tools of production that run flawlessly. Equipment then is in a constant state of readiness with the benefits being the extended life of the equipment, equipment eliminated as a cause of defects, and prevention of major equipment repairs. The four stages of preventative maintenance are breakdown maintenance, preventative maintenance, productive maintenance and total productive maintenance.

Supplier partnerships are a total management and company commitment to a cooperative relationship. This relationship focuses on achieving the lowest total cost through working on non-price areas. The cornerstones of this relationship will be long-term commitments, shared goals and frequent fact-based communications.

Pull systems, often referred to as Kanban, are the mechanisms that activate the production processes. The objectives of the pull system will be threefold: (1) keep the time of producing material as close as possible to the time of using material; (2) maintain accurate and rapid feedback on what is really needed in the work area; and (3) provide local control over stock levels in the area.

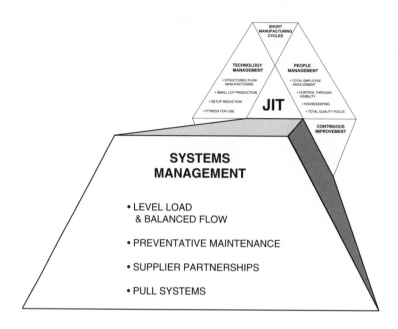

Figure 9-14: Systems Management Elements of JIT

Each manufacturing environment that has been successful at JIT has all 12 of the elements of Just-In-Time in place to one degree or another. It should be noted that the degree of application of the 12 elements in each company can and may be different. For example, in a traditional job shop manufacturer there could be tremendous application of structured flow manufacturing for improved through-put, thus leading to cycle time reduction, while another company that is a process manufacturer already may understand the importance of structured flow manufacturing but may need to focus on preventative maintenance and setup reduction.

RESULTS OF JUST-IN-TIME

Whatever the type of manufacturer or manufacturing process, one thing is certain: working the issues in any company utilizing the 12 elements of Just-In-Time results in short manufacturing cycles, continuous improvement and a total quality focus.

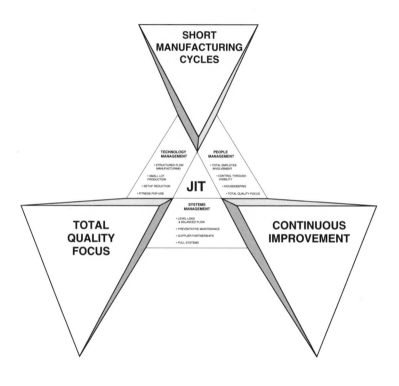

Figure 9-15: Results of JIT

The result of achieving short manufacturing cycles, continuous improvement and a total quality focus is Just-In-Time production. Just-In-Time then is the result rather than the beginning. As companies continue to improve in all elements they achieve a level of precision and exactness that is characterized as Just-In-Time.

131

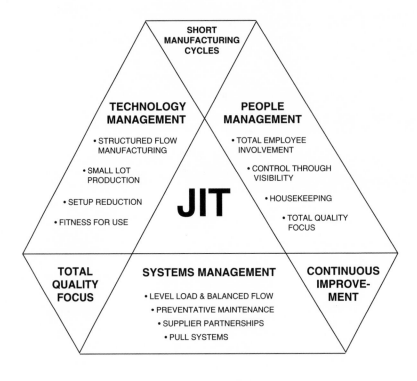

Figure 9-16: JIT Production

CHAPTER 10

Performance Measurement

Performance measurement is the tool that allows a company to understand problem processes, benchmark against other businesses, and ultimately improve. Performance measurement helps to ask the question, "Why?" Asking "Why?" gets to the center of a problem, much like peeling the skin from an onion. Each "why" gets you closer to the core (or problem source). It generally takes at least five "whys" before really understanding the reason.

Performance measurement can have negative connotations, and can give false impressions of management's motives. (Employees sometimes translate performance measurement into targeting employees rather than improving processes.) Having said that, the most important thing to remember is that performance measurement, done correctly, becomes a part of the cultural fiber of the organization and is essential in continuous improvement.

There are generally three phases of performance measurement implementation in most organizations:

1. Denial

The first reaction employees have to performance measurement is denial.

EMPLOYEE: "It's not me! *I'm* not causing the problem. Measure that *other* department – they're the ones that need to get their act together."

Employees can be quite intimidated, wondering what the real motives for these measurements are. The process must be supportive and send the message from management that it is okay to make a mistake on the journey toward improvement. Errors are bound to happen and measures will not always improve every day. If there are not some mistakes happening, the company probably is not trying enough new ideas.

2. Beginning Tolerance

The second phase takes employees into the zone of tolerance.

EMPLOYEE: "Okay, I guess I'll have to do those measurements. I don't have time but I suppose I'll do them anyway. Management doesn't seem to be giving up on the idea."

This is a sign that people are beginning to buy into the process. At this point they have thought about the measurement and probably have assessed the risks. It really is a good sign to see this change in attitude although it is a long way from completely understanding the process.

3. Ownership

The final stage of employees' acceptance of performance measurement comes with the understanding of how these measurements can help the business. Even more important to most employees is how it can make them more efficient and, in most cases, their jobs easier.

Once the process of performance measurement is part of the company's culture and becomes the way the company does business, employees will add constantly to the measurement list.

EMPLOYEE: "I'm not sure we are measuring the right level to solve the problem. I started measuring the 'whatever' and have found it to be more closely linked with the result that consistently causes the barrier that is not letting us improve. I believe we can make adjustments that will improve the condition."

MANAGING WITH PERFORMANCE MEASUREMENTS

The true measure of any new business system implementation is not measured by how many software modules have been implemented, but what happens to the operating performance in the business. Therefore, management must take an active role in identifying problem performance areas and develop action plans to improve or reduce the variation in the process.

Management

> "Management is the activity or task of determining the objectives of an organization and then guiding the people and other resources of the organization in the successful achievement of those objectives."
>
> Marvin Bower
> *The Will To Manage*

Figure 10-1: A Definition of Management

As Marvin Bower defined in his book *The Will To Manage* management is an active process not a passive process. The job is to guide people, resources and the organization in achieving objectives. Utilizing the MRP II business model, management can define operating performance objectives for each area of the business.

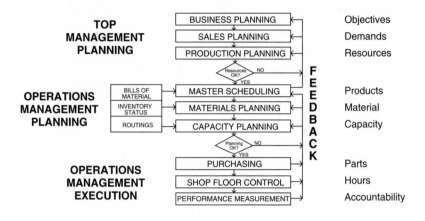

Figure 10-2: The Business Excellence Model

In Chapter 1 we defined Class A MRP II as an operating level of performance of 95% or greater in each area.

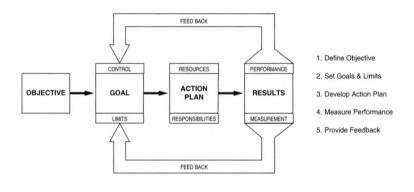

Figure 10-3: Management Cycle

By establishing operating measures management can baseline themselves or measure current performance in business plan performance through delivery performance. If any areas measure below 95% a spin-off task force may be created to map the current process and either improve the process or potentially re-engineer it to achieve

136

higher levels of performance. A performance history can be utilized
to track and measure progress or improved performance in each area
of the MRP II business model.

PERFORMANCE HISTORY YEAR _____

FUNCTIONAL AREA		JAN.	FEB.	MAR.	APR.	MAY	JUNE	JULY	AUG.	SEPT.	OCT.	NOV.	DEC.
TOP MANAGEMENT PLANNING	BUSINESS PLAN												
	SALES PLAN												
	PRODUCTION PLAN												
OPERATIONS MGMT. PLANNING	MASTER SCHEDULE												
	MATERIALS PLAN												
	CAPACITY PLAN												
DATA BASE	BILLS OF MATERIAL												
	INVENTORY CONTROL												
	ROUTINGS												
OPERATIONS MGMT. EXECUTION	PURCHASING												
	SHOP FLOOR CONTROL												
	DELIVERY PERFORMANCE												
PERFORMANCE	TOTAL												
	AVERAGE												
	CLASS												

Figure 10-4: Performance History

Companies on their journey to Class A MRP II visibly display the
performance history for communication and project progress.

An additional important point regarding management and the performance measurement process deals with accountability. A process
owner or owners should be defined for each of the 12 areas in the
business model. In many companies identifying process ownership
for the area or measurement is a significant task in itself.

COMPANY _____ BY _____ DATE _____

	FUNCTIONAL AREA	RESPONSIBILITY	PERFORMANCE OBJECTIVE	PERFORMANCE MEASUREMENT
TOP MANAGEMENT PLANNING	BUSINESS PLAN	GENERAL MANAGER	RETURN ON INVESTMENT	
	SALES PLAN	SALES	SALES PERFORMANCE	
	PRODUCTION PLAN	MANUFACTURING	PRODUCTION PERFORMANCE	
OPERATIONS MANAGEMENT PLANNING	MASTER SCHEDULE	MANUFACTURING	MPS PERFORMANCE	
	MATERIALS PLAN	MATERIALS	SCHEDULE RELIABILITY	
	CAPACITY PLAN	MANUFACTURING	CAPACITY PERFORMANCE	
DATA BASE	BILLS OF MATERIAL	ENGINEERING	BILL OF MATERIAL ACCURACY	
	INVENTORY CONTROL	MATERIALS	INVENTORY ACCURACY	
	ROUTINGS	ENGINEERING	ROUTING ACCURACY	
OPERATIONS MANAGEMENT EXECUTION	PURCHASING	PURCHASING	SCHEDULE PERFORMANCE	
	SHOP FLOOR CONTROL	MANUFACTURING	SCHEDULE PERFORMANCE	
	DELIVERY PERFORMANCE	GENERAL MANAGER	DELIVERY PERFORMANCE	
PERFORMANCE	CLASS	AVERAGE	TOTAL	

Figure 10-5: Performance Report Card

It is difficult to develop the previously discussed action plans and spin-off task forces without proper ownership and accountability for the process. An example might help to illustrate: In many companies when the discussion deals with inventory record accuracy the accounting manager provides information about the accuracy, and accounting is viewed as being responsible for the integrity of the records. The problem here is that accounting cannot be held accountable for performance when they have no control over the process. It is management's responsibility to determine the process owner. In this example of inventory accuracy the true process owner is not accounting but probably is a warehouse/stockroom manager. They have direct control over the people involved with the movement of materials in and out of the stockroom and the associated transactions necessary to maintain accurate inventory records. In this case, and all cases, accounting and information systems normally are support functions, not the real process owner. The important message here is that in most companies significant discussion transpires about defining the process owner even before the discussion on how to measure performance.

CLASS A MRP II MEASUREMENTS

Business Plan

The measure of business plan performance is typically an existing financial measure. Measured monthly these measures could be:

- Return on Investment (ROI)

- Return on Assets (ROA)

- Return on Net Assets (RONA)

- Income to Plan

- Sales Revenue to Plan

- Operating Profit to Plan

The objective of the business plan is to develop the market, product and financial plans for the company. The business plan is the responsibility of the president or general manager and is top management's strategic plan of "what, how much, and when?" for markets, products and profit to meet the company's overall business objectives. The business plan should state dollars of income, dollars of investment and a rate of return on investment for each month and for the year. (Return on assets also is used if investment control is not part of the company business plan.)

FUNCTION	OBJECTIVE	MEASUREMENT
BUSINESS PLAN	INCOME	INCOME = PLAN
RESPONSIBILITY	INVESTMENT	INVESTMENT = PLAN
General Management	RETURN ON INVESTMENT	RETURN ON INVESTMENT = PLAN

Figure 10-6: Business Plan Performance Measurement

The key measurement of the business plan is *return on investment* (ROI). ROI is the percentage derived from the ratio of income over investment. In other words, the income earned from the investment required to support the business plan. Return on investment is useful to evaluate the success of present as well as the potential of new markets and products.

Class A business plan performance is meeting income, investment and return on investment objectives within 5% of plan for a 95% business plan performance.

$$\text{Business Plan Performance \%} = \frac{\text{Actual ROI}}{\text{Planned ROI}} \times 100$$

Sales Plan

The objective of the sales plan is to develop a plan of orders received (bookings) and/or shipments for the company's products. The sales plan is the responsibility of the sales or marketing vice president or department head. The sales plan should be stated in dollars and units by product line by month and for the year. The sales plan is the "what, how much, and when?" of the products required to meet the anticipated customer demand.

The key measurement for the sales plan is *sales plan performance.* Sales management develops the sales plan and it is their responsibility to bring in the orders to meet the plan. Sales plan performance is the orders received as a percent of the planned sales by month.

FUNCTION	OBJECTIVE	MEASUREMENT
SALES PLAN	SALES PLAN REVIEW	SALES PLAN = BUSINESS PLAN BY DOLLAR & UNITS, BY MONTH
RESPONSIBILITY	SALES PLAN PERFORMANCE	ORDERS RECEIVED = SALES PLAN BY DOLLARS BY UNITS, BY MIX BY MONTH
Sales	FINISHED INVENTORY	FINISHED INVENTORY = PLAN BY MONTH

Figure 10-7: Sales Plan Performance Measurement

Class A sales plan performance is meeting the sales dollar plan (by product line) within a 5% tolerance limit for a 95% sales dollar performance, meeting the sales unit plan (by product line) within 10% for a 90% sales unit performance. (The sales mix plan at the master production schedule (MPS) level is often tracked for individual item forecast performance within 15% for an 85% sales mix performance, weekly).

$$\text{Sales Plan Performance \%} = \frac{\text{Orders Received}}{\text{Planned Sales}} \times 100$$

Production Plan

The objective of the production plan is to determine the production rates required to meet the sales plan and maintain a desired level of finished inventory or backlog. The production plan is the responsibility of the manufacturing vice president or department head. It is the "what, how much, and when?" for production rates and levels of output. The production plan should be stated in units of production by product line by month and for the year.

The key measurement is *production plan performance*. Once the production plan has been agreed upon by top management, it is manufacturing's responsibility to produce. Production plan performance is the actual units produced (by product line) as a percentage of planned production by month.

FUNCTION	OBJECTIVE	MEASUREMENT
PRODUCTION PLAN	PRODUCTION PLAN REVIEW	PRODUCTION PLAN = SALES PLAN ± Δ INVENTORY BY MONTH
RESPONSIBILITY	PRODUCTION CAPACITY REVIEW	PRODUCTION RATES CAPACITY CONSTRAINTS PLANNING HORIZON
Manufacturing	PRODUCTION PLAN PERFORMANCE	ACTUAL PRODUCTION = PLAN BY MONTH

Figure 10-8: Production Plan Performance Measurement

Class A production plan performance is meeting the production plan within a 5% tolerance limit for a 95% production plan performance.

$$\text{Production Plan Performance \%} = \frac{\text{Actual Production}}{\text{Planned Production}} \times 100$$

Master Production Schedule

FUNCTION	OBJECTIVE	MEASUREMENT
MASTER PRODUCTION SCHEDULE	MASTER PRODUCTION SCHEDULE REVIEW	SUM OF MASTER PRODUCTION SCHEDULES = MONTHLY PRODUCTION PLAN
RESPONSIBILITY	MASTER PRODUCTION SCHEDULE POLICY	MPS TIME FENCE POLICY MPS CHANGE REVIEW MPS CONSUMPION REVIEW
Materials/ Manufacturing	MASTER PRODUCTION SCHEDULE PERFORMANCE	ACTUAL PRODUCTION = MASTER PRODUCTION SCHEDULE BY UNIT & OPTION BY WEEK

Figure 10-9: Master Production Schedule Performance Measurement

The objective of the master production schedule is to establish the detail product mix to be produced weekly within the monthly product line rates of the production plan. It is the responsibility of materials or manufacturing management. It is the "what, how, much and when?" at the product, model, feature, option or product mix level for scheduling production to meet the sales plan.

The key measurement is *master production schedule performance.* It is the actual units produced as a percentage of units planned to be completed by week.

$$\text{Master Production Schedule Performance \%} = \frac{\text{Actual MPS}}{\text{Planned MPS}} \times 100$$

Class A master production scheduling will produce the product mix within a 5% tolerance limit for a 95% master production schedule performance.

Material Planning

The objective of materials planning is to determine the schedules for parts required to produce the product and to maintain part priorities for production, and is the responsibility of materials management. It is the "what, how much, and when?" of component parts and subassemblies. The materials plan is stated in the manufactured and purchased part schedules required to produce the master production schedule.

FUNCTION	OBJECTIVE	MEASUREMENT
MATERIAL REQUIREMENTS PLANNING	RELEASE RELIABILITY	ON TIME RELEASED VS. TOTAL ORDERS RELEASED
RESPONSIBILITY	MATERIAL AVAILABILITY	MATERIAL AVAILABLE ORDERS VS. TOTAL ORDERS RELEASED
Materials	SCHEDULE RELIABILITY	ORDERS WITH CURRENT DATES VS. TOTAL OPEN ORDERS

Figure 10-10: Materials Planning Performance Measurement

The key measurement is *schedule reliability performance*, which indicates whether orders are being scheduled and rescheduled with current due dates to maintain valid priorities that meet the master production schedule. It measures the reliability of the plan that is being delivered to purchasing and manufacturing on a weekly basis. Schedule reliability is the number of orders with valid due dates as a percentage of the total number of open orders. It can be calculated separately for manufactured and purchased parts planning.

$$\text{Schedule Reliability Performance \%} = \frac{\text{Orders w/Correct Due Dates}}{\text{Total Open Orders}} \times 100$$

Class A materials plan performance is developing a reliable materials plan within a 5% tolerance limit for a 95% schedule reliability performance.

Capacity Planning

The objective of capacity planning is to manage the capacity in labor and machine hours required to produce the product. It is the responsibility of materials management and manufacturing. The capacity plan is the "what, how much and when?" of capacity required to produce the master production schedule. It should be stated in standard hours required to produce the units in the master production schedule by plant, by department and by work center, on a weekly basis.

FUNCTION	OBJECTIVE	MEASUREMENT
CAPACITY REQUIREMENTS PLANNING	CAPACITY PLAN REVIEW	CAPACITY PLAN • BY LOAD CENTER • BY DEPARTMENT • BY PLANT
RESPONSIBILITY		
Manufacturing	INPUT PERFORMANCE	HOURS RELEASED VS. CAPACITY PLAN

Figure 10-11: Capacity Planning Performance Measurement

The key measurement is *capacity plan performance*. The capacity plan should be developed by work center, department, and plant to determine that capacity is available to meet the production plan as well as the weekly master schedule. Capacity plan performance is a weekly measure of the number of hours released (based on standard hours per unit released) as a percentage of the hours planned.

$$\text{Capacity Plan Input Performance \%} = \frac{\text{Hours Released}}{\text{Hours Planned}} \times 100$$

The percentages of each work center are averaged to determine company performance. Class A capacity plan performance is meeting capacity plans within a 5% tolerance limit for a 95% capacity plan performance.

Bills of Material

Bills of material specify the parts or materials and the quantity or amount of each, along with the assembly or process relationships required to produce the product. The bills of material are the responsibility of the engineering function.

FUNCTION	OBJECTIVE	MEASUREMENT
BILL OF MATERIAL	PRODUCT STRUCTURE	PARTS, QUANTITIES LEVEL BY LEVEL FOR ASSEMBLY
RESPONSIBILITY	ENGINEERING CHANGE CONTROL	PLANNED AND ACTUAL EFFECTIVITY DATES
Engineering	OBSOLETE & SURPLUS INVENTORY	OBSOLETE INVENTORY = 5% OF TOTAL INVENTORY

Figure 10-12: Bills of Material Performance Measurement

The key measurement is *bill of material accuracy*, which indicates whether or not the bill of material, as defined in the computer database, represents the product as it is currently being produced. Any error (i.e., any individual component) causes the entire bill to be in error. Bill of material accuracy is the number of single level bills that are in agreement with actual production as a percentage of the total number of single level bills audited.

$$\text{Bill of Material Accuracy \%} = \frac{\text{Bills in Agreement}}{\text{Total Number of Bills Audited}} \times 100$$

Class A bill of material performance is maintaining bill of material accuracy within a 1% tolerance limit for a 99% bill of material accuracy performance.

Inventory Control

The objective of inventory control is to maintain accurate and timely inventory status information. Inventory control is the responsibility of the manager in charge of the stockroom or warehouse. Control cannot be achieved, however, without every employee understanding the importance of accurate inventories and their contribution to achieve them.

FUNCTION	OBJECTIVE	MEASUREMENT
INVENTORY CONTROL	INVENTORY ACCURACY	PHYSICAL COUNT VS. INVENTORY RECORD
RESPONSIBILITY		
Materials	INVENTORY MANAGEMENT	INVENTORY INVESTMENT = INVENTORY PLAN

Figure 10-13: Inventory Control Performance Measurement

The key measurement is *inventory record accuracy*, which indicates the accuracy of the on-hand inventory record as compared to the physical inventory (part number by location). The count is either right or wrong, within agreed-upon tolerance limits. Only parts that need to be weighed or scale counted will have a tolerance different than 0%. Inventory record accuracy is the number of parts, by location, where the physical count equals the inventory record as a percentage of the total number of parts counted.

$$\text{Inventory Record Accuracy \%} = \frac{\text{Number of Parts Correct}}{\text{Number of Parts Counted}} \times 100$$

Class A inventory control performance is maintaining inventory accuracy within a 5% tolerance limit for 95% inventory accuracy performance.

Routings

Routings specify the operations that must be performed to produce the product. Routings are the responsibility of manufacturing, manufacturing engineering and industrial engineering. The routing should specify the sequence of operations, the machine or work center, the tooling or fixtures, process instructions, and the setup and run hours for each operation.

FUNCTION	OBJECTIVE	MEASUREMENT
ROUTING	WORK CENTER ACCURACY	WORK CENTER DEFINITION
RESPONSIBILITY	OPERATION SEQUENCE ACCURACY	OPERATION SEQUENCING
Engineering	METHOD & STANDARDS ACCURACY	METHODS & STANDARDS

Figure 10-14: Routings Performance Measurement

The key measurement is *routing accuracy*. Routing accuracy indicates whether the routing, as defined in the computer database, represents the sequence of operations as they are actually performed in production areas. Any error in a routing (i.e., any individual operation) causes the entire routing to be in error. Routing accuracy is the number of routings that are in agreement with the actual production methods as a percentage of the total routings audited.

$$\frac{\text{Routing}}{\text{Accuracy \%}} = \frac{\text{Routings in Agreement}}{\text{Total Routings Audited}} \times 100$$

Class A routing accuracy is maintaining routing accuracy within a 5% tolerance limit for a 95% routing accuracy.

Purchasing

The objective of purchasing is to deliver purchased materials on the date needed with the required quality and best price (cost). Purchasing plan performance is the responsibility of purchasing management. It is the detailed "what, how much, and when?" for purchased materials, parts, and services to execute the plan. The purchasing plan is stated in purchased items required to be delivered daily, in order to achieve the master production schedule.

FUNCTION	OBJECTIVE	MEASUREMENT
PURCHASING	SCHEDULE PERFORMANCE	DELIVERY DATE VS. DUE DATE
RESPONSIBILITY	PURCHASE ORDER RELEASE	SCHEDULE RELEASE VS. QUANTITY BUY ORDER
Purchasing	PURCHASE DOLLAR RECEIPTS	DOLLAR RECEIPTS VS. PLAN

Figure 10-15: Purchasing Performance Measurement

The key measurement is *schedule performance*. Schedule performance indicates whether purchasing is delivering purchased material or parts on the date needed by manufacturing. It is the number of purchased items delivered as a percentage of the purchased items due, daily.

$$\text{Purchasing Schedule Performance \%} = \frac{\text{Items Delivered}}{\text{Items Due}} \times 100$$

Class A purchasing performance delivers purchased material to the day scheduled within a 5% tolerance limit for a 95% purchasing performance.

Shop Floor Control

The objective of shop floor control is to produce a sufficient quantity of manufactured parts on the date needed to meet the master production schedule. Shop floor control is the responsibility of manufacturing. It is the daily execution of the "what, how much, and when?" of labor and material in the manufacturing facility.

FUNCTION	OBJECTIVE	MEASUREMENT
SHOP FLOOR CONTROL	SCHEDULE PERFORMANCE	COMPLETION DATE VS. DUE DATE
RESPONSIBILITY	OUTPUT PERFORMANCE	ACTUAL OUTPUT VS. PLANNED OUTPUT
Manufacturing	PRODUCTIVITY PERFORMANCE	PRODUCTIVITY VS. PLAN

Figure 10-16: Shop Floor Control Performance Measurement

The key measurement is *schedule performance*. Schedule performance indicates whether manufacturing parts are being completed on time in the shop. Schedule performance is a daily measure of the number of parts manufactured as a percentage of the total number of parts due and available at that work center. Shop floor control performance is stated in terms of work center schedule performance or assembly line schedule performance.

$$\text{Manufacturing Schedule Performance \%} = \frac{\text{Operations Complete}}{\text{Total Operations Due}} \times 100$$

Class A shop floor control performance meets daily manufacturing schedules with a 5% tolerance limit for a 95% shop floor control performance.

Schedule Performance

The objective of schedule performance is to build the product on time, ship the product on time, and deliver the product to the customer when it was promised. It is the "what, how much and when?" in units delivered to meet the sales plan. Since schedule performance in delivery is dependent on the entire company working together, the responsibility for this measure rests with the president or general manager.

FUNCTION	OBJECTIVE	MEASUREMENT
DELIVERY PERFORMANCE	BUILD PERFORMANCE	ACTUAL BUILD VS. PLAN
RESPONSIBILITY	SHIP PERFORMANCE	ACTUAL SHIP VS. PLAN
General Manager	DELIVERY PERFORMANCE	DELIVERY VS. PROMISE

Figure 10-17: Schedule Performance Measurement

The key measurement is *delivery performance*. It measures whether the product was shipped to the customer on the date promised. Delivery performance is the number of items shipped on time as a percentage of the total number of items shipped. "On time" implies that item quality has been confirmed, directly or indirectly.

$$\frac{\text{Delivery}}{\text{Performance \%}} = \frac{\text{Orders/Items Shipped on Time}}{\text{Total Orders/Items Shipped}} \times 100$$

Class A schedule performance promises and delivers the product on time within a 5% tolerance limit for a 95% schedule performance Level.

BEYOND CLASS A

As the business moves toward Class A MRP II with 95% performance in each of the previously defined 12 areas, performance is predictable and the whole company operates to the plan. So what is next?

DETAIL PERFORMANCE MEASUREMENTS

In World Class Manufacturing the focus is on continuous improvement. Measurements in place should, therefore, activate improvements. Management evaluates the measurement process based upon the rate of improvement. The measurements are designed to drive the improvement process in the critical elements of quality, cost, flexibility, reliability and innovation. The measurements we have seen and recommend for companies striving for World Class levels are as follows:

Quality

1) Percent reduction in total cost of quality.

2) Percent reduction in defects.

3) Percent of certified suppliers.

4) Percent reduction in supplier base.

5) Percent reduction in time between defect occurrence, detection and correction.

Cost

1) Percent increase in inventory turnover.

2) Percent reduction in data transactions.

3) Percent increase in materials shipped to point of use by supplier.

4) Percent increase in dollars of output per employee.

5) Percent reduction in floor space utilized.

Flexibility

1) Percent reduction in cycle time.

2) Percent reduction in setup time.

3) Percent reduction in lot/batch size.

4) Percent increase in number of jobs mastered per employee.

5) Percent increase in common materials used per product.

Reliability

1) Percent increase of process capable equipment.

2) Percent increase in overall equipment effectiveness.

3) Percent reduction in product or service warranty costs.

4) Percent reduction in engineering changes.

5) Percent increase in on-time delivery.

Innovation

1) Percent reduction in new product introduction lead time.

2) Percent increase in new product sales revenue was a percent of total sales revenue.

3) Percent increase in number of new patents granted.

4) Customer perception of the company as a leader in innovation.

5) Percent of management time spent on leading or fostering innovation.

CHAPTER 11

Implementing MRP II: The Ten Steps to Success

The most challenging component of MRP II implementations is getting started. Knowing the philosophy of MRP II and understanding the concepts of predictable performance and accurate planning is quite different from understanding how to put the pieces in place to introduce the kinds of change that affect not only the processes and procedures but also the culture. Few Class A operations can truthfully report a smooth start-up with no snags whatsoever. It is a major change for most organizations and it requires everyone to stretch their comfort zone.

While there are no magic bullets, there are proven steps that have been repeated at Class A MRP II implementations. Let there be no doubt that the first step is understanding the benefits that can be derived from the improvement. Without this knowledge employee buy-in is missing and while it is possible to implement change without massive formal training, it puts a tremendous strain on relations within the company and moves the timeline out months, maybe years, before benefits are realized. Ultimately the benefits do not start until all people in the organization are working together, understand the objectives, and have some basic idea of how to accomplish those objectives. The initial training and education, provided up front in the implementation provides the shortest path to realization of predictable, continuously improved performance. It is routine how many Class A organizations, when asked if they would do anything differently, say they would do more education up front — although they did what they considered to be a lot at the time.

The key elements or steps to a successful implementation are:

1. Education & Leadership
2. Guidance
3. Performance Measurement
4. Accountability
5. Handshake Management
6. Project Team and Leader
7. Cost/Benefit Justification
8. Project Plan
9. Database Integrity
10. Hardware and Software

Each of these steps represents a major commitment within the company, from the CEO to the rank and file.

STEP 1: EDUCATION & LEADERSHIP

Leadership is one of the most critical factors in the successful implementation of Class A MRP II. In our surveys over the last fifteen years of working with and interviewing Class A companies, every one of the companies had a senior manager championing the MRP II implementation. In 100% of the Class A companies, a senior manager was the champion of the change effort. Preferably, the senior management champion should be the president or person in charge of the business. Why? The MRP II implementation cuts across the entire organization and there is only one person with the authority to organize the resources or ensure the changes are implemented in each area, and that is at the top of the organization.

It is important to understand that the MRP II implementation is not just the responsibility of the person in charge of the business. It is the job/responsibility of all senior managers. Mr. John Teets, Chairman of the Dial Corporation, once stated "management's job is to not view the business as it is today, but what it needs to be in the future." This is precisely the role of all senior managers in the MRP II effort. Senior management cannot be the defender of the "status quo" but now must work everyday to sell the organization and its departments on the MRP II concepts. For example, the manufacturing manager can no longer just be concerned with reviewing daily performance on production and shipments. He or she now must be just as concerned with inventory and bill of material accuracy.

The education process for Class A MRP II is broken into three steps or phases. The first phase is top management education. This is also the area where most companies that are not successful in their implementation compromise their effort. This is due to senior management's view of the MRP II project. These views are traditionally, "Why do I need to be trained in the software?" or "This effort does not really impact me or my area because this new computer system is for manufacturing and operations people." To answer these responses one must first understand the difference between education and training. Education in an MRP II effort is about what MRP II is and how it applies to the business and the changes in the current management practices that will be required to achieve higher levels of performance in business operations. The training will be related to the hardware and software. It is the, "How does the system work?" or "How do we complete an inventory transaction using the new system versus our current system?" This training on the system should be conducted by the firm from whom the software was purchased.

The most successful approach to top management education is for the top management to attend a course (typically 2-3 days) about the subject of MRP II. This phase of the education should cover the concepts of Class A MRP II, how these concepts apply to the company, the changes required to make it happen, senior management's role in the implementation, performance measurements for Class A MRP II and the steps to success. The most successful approach in the top management education is to go through the education as a team. By doing the education as a team a consensus and common vision as to how to move forward as a company (action plan) can be formulated.

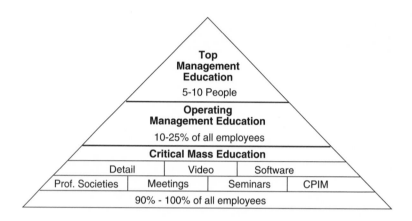

Figure 11-1: Education Pyramid

The second phase of the education is for operating management. The operating management education typically is for 10-25% of the organization and should be started no later than 30 days after the top management education. The education should encompass department managers, first line supervision, project team members and key staff/support. The operating education is normally a two-day course taught by outside instructors off-site from the company with cross-functional representation from each area of the business. For example, if there are 200 employees in the company, 10-25% of the organization would mean 20-35 people should attend the two-day course on Class A MRP II. Having these people attend as a group will cut 3-6 months off the length of the project. Also, for many companies, it is the first time in the history of the business that education has been done cross-functionally. Typically, most companies educate by function. For example, sales goes to classes on sales, finance goes to classes on finance, etc.

Again, why is the operating management education important? Our experience has shown that 100% of the companies that were not successful in their implementations fail because they cannot push the new ideas, concepts and ways of operating through either the top management of the company or the operating management. In other words, this project never fails because of lack of acceptance at the factory floor level. Do not underestimate the challenge!

The third phase in the education process is the critical mass education. In Class A MRP II companies 100% of the organization receives some form of education and training. After all, what is Class A MRP II about? It is about reinvesting in the people, raising the technical competence throughout the organization, not just implementing software.

Educating and training 100% of the workforce can be broken down into pieces. Detailed education should transpire based upon need or operating performance. For example, if inventory record accuracy is an important issue then detailed education on inventory accuracy would be required. The same could be said for bills of material, setup reduction and sales, operations planning to name a few.

Probably the most cost-effective method for educating the organization is through the use of video-based education. It is important to understand, however, that video education is not just putting people in a room and having them watch a screen. That is a recipe for certain failure. Watching video is basically information and fact transfer. Studies show that retention after simply watching and listening to someone talk, (i.e., a video) is 50% or less.

The most effective video-based education is comprised of three elements:

1. Video Tape

This is the presentation of the concept in a 15-18 minute video. Information and facts regarding the concept are shown. Normal attendance for a video session is 10-15 employees.

2. Workbook Exercises

The retention level is always higher when the student has an opportunity to practice the concept. Work exercises and case studies in the workbook are the ideal format.

3. Application

Once the concepts have been presented through the video and work exercises to ensure understanding the next step in the learning process is application. Here is where discussion and action plans are developed. For example, discussion should center on how the concept presented in the video applies to our business or, more importantly, how would we make this concept happen in our company? This third part provides closure on the learning experience.

Video is viewed as the catalyst to bring people together in the company to work on performance improvement. Class A companies use video in a focused business meeting approach. In these focused business meetings or video sessions the instructors should be department managers and project team members. The reasons for department managers and project team members as instructors are simple: (1) the manager is now positioned as the change agent or supporter of the new order of things, and (2) the operations people are likewise positioned as being accountable for making the items or actions discussed actually happen. Resist the temptation to set up one individual as the trainer/educator for taking all personnel through the video, because there is no accountability for that person (the trainer) in making what is talked about in the sessions really happen.

Many different education techniques have been tried while implementing MRP II. The best way requires the most commitment. Companies that hurry the education or are "indecisive" or "timid" about how much importance they put on attendance of the "busy" people of the organization in classes see little real gain. These companies still spend the time and money required to facilitate the classes, but the benefits are minimized because of poor attendance and lack of management commitment. These "busy" people who miss class are often either the informal leaders or the formal leaders in the organization. The frustrations they currently experience will continue; the changes will not make sense to them initially; and the initiative will not have their full support. These energetic people can become antibodies to change, something to be avoided at every opportunity. After all, these are good, dedicated people we are talking about. They do not and will not understand without experience or exposure to education. Some of the ideas will seem radical until the results are obvious and real.

Be aware from the outset that education will continue forever beyond this start-up phase of the project. While it is more often administered in blocks, budgeting a minimum of 2% of the labor time on average, or approximately 45 minutes per week per person, is minimum for maintaining Class A environments once the initial education has been completed. Initial education should be much more than 2% and can be as much as 25% for project team members. Expenditures on education in the organization should be the last item to be considered as discretionary.

STEP 2: GUIDANCE

Consultants can play a necessary part in the process of improvement. Without outside guidance, too much can be left to the individual internal influence with the most power, loudest voice, or most persistence. It only can be hoped that these characteristics combine with the most knowledge. It is coincidental when they do.

Project managers in MRP II implementations find that there are many lessons at the project team level that are understood over time but not well understood within top management. These might include issues related to software requirements, database management, educational needs, policy change requirements. Creative ideas can be radical, necessitating top management buy-in. With outside sources who have seen similar ideas tried at other companies, they can advise for or against with experience to back up their views, and can arrange networking between top managers of other firms.

Change happens at what can be an alarming rate during an MRP II implementation. Most companies find they can use all the help they can get. The costs are minimal considering the returns are so great, and companies without outside resources require a much longer average development time to reach Class A. Competition is pushing at an increasing rate. By studying other people's mistakes through an outside expert's eyes, the company can minimize the lessons "the hard way" and make the most efficient transition.

Getting outside help does not always mean just utilizing consultants. Outside help should be looked at as a way to educate and save time and money in the implementation process. For example, visiting other companies can save time, money and be educational. If the company has inventory accuracy problems there might be other companies within driving distance that had the same problem. Visiting the outside company provides a chance to interact with others who have solved the problem. The old adage of "a picture is worth a thousand words" is still true today. Visit other companies. Ask them how they did it, what they did wrong, what were the major obstacles to success, what would be done differently if the company was going through the exercise again. When the company provides information, write it down. Also, take pictures (if they permit them).

Another key form of outside guidance that is beneficial are professional societies. There are a number of professional societies that provide excellent low cost education and an opportunity to network and be exposed to other businesses. All of these are involved in furthering the body of knowledge in manufacturing and disseminating best practices.

If a company intends to use outside an consultant, the consultant's job should not be to come in and do the company's work for them. There has been very limited success in hiring consultants to be in the company full time to implement MRP II; however, there has been much more success using consultants to work with the company's senior management, project team and spin-off task forces involved in the MRP II implementation. The role of the consultant is to help the company stay focused on the right goals and activities and in the proper sequence. Their job is to help set objectives, help with the technical obstacles that are encountered and help measure performance. The consultant should "resist the temptation to pick up the pencil and do the work for the company." Their role is to not make the company dependent on them but make the company capable of doing the work for themselves.

STEP 3: PERFORMANCE MEASUREMENT

As discussed in Chapter 10, "Performance Measurements", the true measure of Class A Manufacturing Resource Planning is not whether new systems have been implemented, but what happened to the operating performance in the business. The focus then is on operating performance, not just financial performance. Just measuring financial performance is like driving your car through the rear-view mirror. By the time the numbers show up on the income statement and balance sheet it is after the fact; it has already happened. With a good set of operating performance measures obtained by the MRP II process in place a company can take corrective action before it impacts the financial statement.

The performance measurements in place should focus on rates of improvement to drive the habit of ongoing or continuous improvement. Management also should look at performance measurement as a way to highlight or provide focus on the problem performance areas. Obviously, in the quest for Class A MRP II areas below 95% performance require an action plan to improve the performance.

Measurement review meetings must take place on a weekly basis at the execution phase and monthly at the business plan, sales plan, and production plan levels.

STEP 4: ACCOUNTABILITY

The most effective way to create the necessary accountability in the improvement process is to have regularly scheduled review meetings chaired by the process owner. The process owner is not always the person to execute the plan, but instead, the person to help, and the one who has responsibility to drive the improvement process for that particular area.

The process of review is effective if done with a schedule similar to the following:

A. First day of month:
Bookings/Sales Forecast Review Meeting

This meeting is chaired by sales/marketing and is a review of the preceding month's bookings or forecast to plan. Sales is responsible for reconciling the inaccuracies, if any, in the sales plan and providing an updated plan. The master scheduler and manufacturing manager describe the effects on lead time or lost production capacity slots, if any, due to the bookings/sales variations from plan.

B. First day of week:
Performance Review Meeting

Chaired by the operations manager and attended by production and materials personnel, this meeting is held to report the weekly measurements (master schedule, inventory accuracy, bill of material, routing accuracy, materials, capacity, purchasing, schedule, performance and customer service). The measurements are reported by the people responsible for the area. These measurements change from time to time depending on the degree of success in improvement. It is common for new measurements to be added frequently. Others are eliminated when they have been at 95% of plan for some time and are deemed to be no longer useful.

C. First week of month:
Top Management Operational Review Meeting

Top management meets to review the business plan, sales plan, and production plan. These measurements should be reported by the top managers in charge of finance, sales, and production, respectively. Holding these managers responsible for these measurements is the responsibility of the top manager (CEO, president, general manager, etc.) in the facility.

Also, at this meeting the realigned production plan is reviewed with the changes that came from the bookings/sales forecast review meeting. Such changes affect the business plan, sales plan, production plan and inventory/backlog plans.

D. Daily:
Production Meeting

This review by materials planners and supervisors regarding the daily dispatch list or daily schedule is typically a 15-minute stand-up meeting to maintain the validity of the daily schedule. Discussion centers on jobs due for the day, will they be completed, are there other hot jobs, or do jobs need to be rescheduled and what are the implications of the pull in or reschedule out?

STEP 5: HANDSHAKE MANAGEMENT

When an organization decides to make the commitment to implement MRP II, it commits to major changes, new ways of doing things, and new ways of thinking. There will be excitement generated, and in the best environment creativity will flourish. If the general population within the organization is risk averse, positive change will not happen as it should. The way to ensure the most creativity is to create an environment where people are coached and expected to take some chances with new ideas that are anticipated to make a positive influence. The resulting enthusiasm can become dynamic.

Management must display a positive attitude supporting empowerment. This means giving the authority to initiate change, allowing it, and rewarding it. This is "handshake management", the antonym of "foxhole management". Symptoms of foxhole management include waiting to prey on employees who make a mistake regardless of the motivation behind it. Blame or finger pointing is an important goal in foxhole activity.

Figure 11-2: Foxhole Management

Keep the focus on opportunity and the future, not on blame and the past. Handshake management is making the decisions based upon fact rather than emotion. It is focusing on the process not the person. As W.E. Deming once said, "everyone wants to do a good job: it is the process that we have in place that prevents and frustrates the workforce." Besides taking a process orientation to improvement, company management must be prepared to make mistakes in the improvement process. In other words, not every thing or every new idea will work. The question then becomes one of company culture: Is it all right to propose new ideas and potentially make mistakes? Or is the culture one where, when mistakes are made, there is finger-pointing and a search for the guilty?

STEP 6: PROJECT TEAM AND LEADER

The project leader and team are integral to the success of the implementation. The project manager should be selected using the following criteria:

1. The individual should be well respected by the rank and file.

It works best if he or she has been with the organization, understands the company's products and processes, and is trusted by the other employees.

2. The project manager should be a leader.

The person should be a self-starter, work well with others, and have an ability to understand the general business direction. The project manager, due to the reporting relationship with senior management, should be looked upon as a peer by the executive management team. The project manager must be able to sit in with top management and provide candid feedback to them on their involvement in the project and the key areas of improvement in developing top management plans. In fact, if the project manager selected is not already part of senior management, the MRP II implementation should be looked upon as one of the steps through which he/she will become a member of senior management in the company's succession plans.

3. The project manager position should be full-time and the person the company can least afford to take out of their current position.

The only way the MRP II project will have the support and focus it needs is to have someone driving the process full-time who has backing and support from top management. Many companies have tried to do it with part-time project managers, but few have been successful.

Why a full-time project manager? First of all, any job worth doing is worth one full-time person or do not write it down as an objective. Companies that compromise on picking the best person for project manager and how much time they devote to the project typically can be traced back to priorities in the company. By not allocating the best person full time the company essentially is assigning

167

and signaling to the rest of the organization that the MRP II project has a lot lower priority than other goals or projects. The companies that achieve Class A MRP II will say the project was the number one priority in the business (other than shipping product).

The project manager should report very high in the organization. Most companies have the project manager report directly to the CEO or president. Do not have the project manager report levels down in the organization. Again, this sends the message that the project has a low priority. The MRP II project cuts across all functional areas and there is only one place in the organization where that happens in a company - at the top!

With an objective to manage all the resources in the business enterprise the project team should have representation from the entire organization.

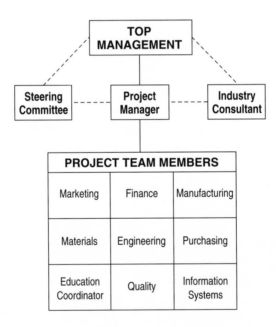

Figure 11-3: Project Organization

The team members will report to the project manager with a dotted line reporting structure while still reporting to their existing functional managers in daily activities. The role of the project team members is as follows:

A. Meet on a weekly basis for approximately $1-1\frac{1}{2}$ hours to review status of the project plan.

B. Lead spin-off task forces that are developed to address the operating performance problems in the business. Typical spin-off task forces that are developed:

    • Inventory Accuracy

    • Bills of Material & Routings

    • Sales and Operations Planning

    • Shop Floor/Just-In-Time (JIT)

The spin-off task forces meet at least weekly. Their activities could be education, training, mapping current processes and developing changes in policies and procedures to ensure improved performance.

C. Provide and lead the education and training effort for those who work within the respective team members' span of control.

Again, remember — the selection criteria of team members for the MRP II project is not based upon who is available. Apply the same logic in the selection process for team members as was done for the project manager. It should be pointed out. however, that team members typically are not full time. They are the future leaders and senior managers in the organization. The MRP II project should be looked at by senior managers as a way and opportunity to reinvest in the company leaders of tomorrow.

The steering committee consists of president/CEO and direct reports. They meet at least monthly with the project manager to review overall project status. In the project plan (to be discussed later in this chapter) there should be key benchmarks or milestones by quartile. These benchmarks or milestones can assist senior management with the major tasks. For example, the steering committee

169

should be focusing on subjects such as inventory accuracy, when it is to be achieved, the resources required and the obstacles to success. The spin-off task force, out of the project team for inventory accuracy, should be working on items such as control groups for cycle counting and tolerances for item counts.

STEP 7: COST/BENEFIT JUSTIFICATION

Part of the project is understanding the reason for the high priority Class A companies put on the implementation effort. One of the first tasks or assignments of the project team must be to cost justify the implementation. By the mere assignment from top management to the project team, top management has acknowledged that it believes there is justification for the expenditure of resource and money, but the team and functional managers must personally sign up for the benefits. This means listing, quantifying, and scheduling benefits. Justifications typically and realistically include:

Costs
A. Education and training
B. Outside consulting services
C. Facilitator training and resource
D. Full time project manager
E. Some travel for company visits
F. Time spent on the project by team members
G. Training aids, books, video materials, etc.
H. Software and hardware (depending on need)

Benefits
A. Achieving data accuracy
B. Inventory reduction
C. Delivery performance improvement
D. Improved flexibility through setup reduction and cycle time reduction
E. Improved product quality
F. Improved morale/quality of life for employees

G. Reduced purchasing and traffic costs

H. Increased sales from increased competitiveness

I. Improved productivity

Sales Volume	$25 Million	$50 Million	$100 Million
Education	$65,000	$85,000	$140,000
Industry Consultant	40,000	50,000	60,000
Software	110,000	240,000	350,000
Hardware	140,000	250,000	500,000
Peoplepower	160,000	360,000	550,000
Total Costs	**$515,000**	**$985,000**	**$1,600,000**

Figure 11-4: Typical Implementation Costs

Sales Volume	$25 Million	$50 Million	$100 Million
Inventory Reduction	$500,000	$1,000,000	$2,000,000
Purchasing & Traffic	150,000	300,000	600,000
Scrap / Rework	225,000	450,000	900,000
Productivity Improvement	200,000	400,000	800,000
Customer Service	250,000	500,000	1,000,000
Total Benefits	**$1,325,000**	**$2,650,000**	**$5,300,000**

Figure 11-5: Typical Implementation Benefits

SALES VOLUME	$25 MILLION	$50 MILLION	$100 MILLION
Costs	$515,000	$985,000	$1,600,000
Benefits	$1,325,000	$2,650,000	$5,300,000

Figure 11-6: Costs vs. Benefits Comparison

In the illustration of a 50 million dollar company example there are several key points. On the cost side certain rules of thumb seem to apply in the companies achieving Class A MRP II. They are:

Education and Consulting	10-15% of the project cost
Hardware & Software	40-50% of the project cost
People	35-40% of the project cost

Because the people cost is not hiring new people but is the project manager's and team members' time, the people cost is not an out of pocket expense.

On the benefit side in the company illustrated, again there are rules of thumb or ranges being achieved in Class A MRP II companies. They are:

Inventory Reduction	25-50%
Purchased Material Cost Reduction	2-10%
Scrap/Rework/Obsolescence	50-100%
Productivity Increase	10-15%
Increased Sales	10-20%

The company illustration also calculates the return on investment (ROI) for the project. The cost for every month the project is not completed (cost of a one-month delay) could be calculated by taking the benefits and dividing by 12 (months). This gives senior management what it is costing the business every month the project is not completed. Class A MRP II companies are achieving at least a 250% return on investment in the project. It also is important to note that the costs for Class A and non-Class A companies are approximately the same. The difference between the Class A and non-Class A is the allocation of funds. The non-Class A companies tend to spend little on education and consulting but spend more on software, presumably to modify it.

STEP 8: PROJECT PLAN

The project plan is an important undertaking for the team, but once done, it represents a constitution that can provide needed guidance along the way. That is not to say there will not be major revisions to it as the team and organization gets further into the project. There will be many updates and revisions going into and beyond Class A certification.

The team should be charged with the task of mapping the course of attack. A recommended way to begin the project planning process is with the ten steps in this chapter. These are main components that must be dealt with in the implementation of MRP II and will serve well as the nucleus of the plan.

The project plan should be broken into the following components:

Mission Statement

The mission statement agreed to by the project team and steering committee should define the scope and objectives of the project.

TEAM MISSION STATEMENT

To guide the organization to a level of basic business
excellence where there is a one plan process, and all functions
are integrated through the formal new business system.
To accomplish this task, it is understood that in all business
areas performance must be a minimum of 95% performance.

Upon completion of the one plan process being established
with 95%+ performance in each business area,
the responsibility of the operational excellence team will be
to begin to move the organization to a process of continuous
improvement leading to operational excellence.

By accomplishing these goals we will position our corporation
to operate with the highest level of reliability, flexibility,
competitiveness and responsiveness possible
for total internal and external customer satisfaction.

Figure 11-7: Sample Mission Statement

173

Operating Plan

The operational component of the project plan deals with the specific tasks, time frames and responsibilities to improve the operating performance in the business. This portion of the plan is often the most overlooked component of the project plan. The vast majority of MRP II implementations have a very detailed plan to implement new software. But there is nothing written into the plan about how performance will be improved, the time frame in which it will be improved, the ownership or responsibility, and the specific actions required to improve the performance in a given area or process. (In Appendix B, the Buker, Inc. milestone methodology provides the general framework to produce the operational portion of the project plan. In Appendix C, a sample company operational plan is available.)

An age old example of defining an operational plan would be achieving inventory record accuracy. New software in and of itself will not improve inventory accuracy. To improve the accuracy of the data a plan must be developed. That plan normally includes steps like mapping the process (the IS condition), developing a cycle count routine starting with a control group, defining tolerances for items to be cycle counted, audit routines to track down the errors, defined time frames to improve the accuracy and ownership of the plan.

System Implementation Plan

This portion of the plan defines how the new business system will be implemented. Like the operational plan there should be a definition of tasks, time frames, and responsibilities. The systems implementation plan normally is developed by information technology and project operating personnel. In the development of the plan there would be a number of considerations: Is an existing software system being replaced? Will the software be implemented on a module by module basis? How will the conference room pilot be set up? After the conference room pilot, will the live implementation start with a product line pilot implementation? These are just some of the questions to be addressed by the team as they put together a plan to implement the new business system.

There are several software conversion methods. The first is known as *cold turkey*, which is defined by turning off the old system on Friday night, loading the data over the weekend, and switching the new system on Monday. The cold turkey approach is dangerous and normally has a great amount of pain associated with it. People are not experienced with the new software but have to keep customers happy without knowing how to utilize the system fully. This can cause frustration that often is blamed on the software when training might well be the issue. This initial perception of the system can last a long time and is certainly not desirable.

A second method is the *parallel approach*. Here companies try to run two systems, the old one and the new one, in parallel for a while to confirm the accuracy of the new and to insure themselves against shutting down the plant because the new system does not do what was expected. This method is difficult because it requires synchronization. Keeping two databases in sync is very difficult in the best environments.

It is also difficult to get people to utilize the new system fully when the old comfortable one is there to depend on. This slows up real learning and ownership. The result is often very close to the cold turkey approach when the conversion actually happens since the new system is not challenged prior to conversion.

The most common software implementation is to start with the *conference room pilot*. This method gets its name because the team selected to implement the software sets up a simulated business in a conference room using the new software. These selected members are key individuals within the organization and have the experience to make sound decisions.

All transactions that are required to run a manufacturing company are simulated as realistically as possible in the conference room pilot. The new software and hardware is wired into the room and each team member has a function within the company simulation.

The first action is to test the system switches. These switches are software choices that are critical to the workings of the system once it is installed live. Decisions have to be made as to how the company wants the software to handle specific situations. Some choices might include costing decisions, transactions to relieve inventory, performance measurement parameters, billing generation, order entry configuration, and a myriad of other possibilities.

Generally, the conference room pilot team will begin by making up random and imaginary bill structures and transactions to get a feel for the processes. Later, a major piece of the data base structure will be moved from real life into the pilot to begin simulating the company in a more realistic mode. By this time, the team members are getting more and more proficient on the system and are starting to work out details and procedures where the new software handles things differently from the existing system. It is important to work out these details while customers are not being negatively affected.

After a total simulation can be performed from order entry to manufacturing to billing, pilot runs should be completed.

Going Live — Once the conference room pilot team has satisfied the testing of the software and written the policies surrounding its use, determined the positioning of software switches, trained the employees, and successfully demonstrated a pilot to management, it is time for the real thing. Going live still has risk involved, even for those who have done the most thorough job in the conference room pilot. Risks come from situations in real life that were not thoroughly tested and thought through in the pilot. There is so much variability in real life, it is difficult to test every possible combination of situations. The goal is to minimize risk.

When the team and the facility are ready, one of two approaches can be used to make the transition to the new software after a pilot run. One approach is to go live with the entire facility, keeping the pilot team intact for a few weeks to act as the team to help employees when they have questions, concerns, or problems.

Another method is to take a part of the business such as one product line or assembly area, and move all planning and execution of that defined piece of business to the new software. The pilot team stays intact to manage this part of the business with help from the employees regularly involved with these products and schedules. The advantage to this approach is the limited amount of risk. The disadvantage is that it takes longer to get the complete software transition completed which can translate into increased costs as duplication in some functions is created. Areas such as accounting and sales are required to utilize two systems which causes increases in resource requirements. The decision has to be made with regard to the particular environment, management, training, and existing software system. Another consideration is company size.

Software conversion is not an easy task and should not be taken lightly. Much thought and education should be exercised prior to deciding to implement a new business system. If the business makes the decision to convert, it is wise to stick with a few reputable software suppliers and keep the package as generic as possible for the short term.

Education and Training Plan

As discussed in Step 1, the companies that are successful in their implementation educate and train 100% of the workforce. A phased education and training plan should be developed so everyone receives some form of education and training.

Sample Project: Team Video-Based Education

What: Project Team Education
Who: Jan Doe (Project Manager)

1. VIDEOPLUS® MRP II series, 80 hours class time
        Start: January 3
        Complete: February 28
2. Company visits
    a. Company X
        Start: Mar 15
        Complete: Mar 15
    b. Company Y
        Start: June 1
        Complete: June 1
    c. Company Z
        Start:
        Complete:
3. Additional Focus Classes - 8 hours class time
    a. Bill of Materials Class
        Start: Mar 15
        Complete: Mar 15
    b. Data Accuracy Class
        Start: Apr 15
        Complete: April 15
    c. Just-In-Time Class
        Start: May 15
        Complete: May 15
4. Required Reading
        Start: Jan 3
        Complete: Ongoing

STEP 9: DATA INTEGRITY

As stated earlier in Chapter 7, data accuracy is a prerequisite to any successful decision making process. Decisions are made every minute within an organization using data gathered in the many databases maintained by the business. If these decisions are to be the best possible, the information has to be accurate and timely. When data is not reliable, typically one of two actions results. Either the users are aware of the data inadequacy and compensate with buffer (not the best decision under any circumstances) or if the users do not acknowledge the shortfall in accuracy, the decision they make may be wrong. Either way the company enjoys something less than desirable results.

The objective is to have the data maintenance done cost-effectively and accurately, and to be able to make decisions without human interaction whenever possible. This is a main focus of an MRP II implementation and a major segment of the project plan.

STEP 10: TOOLS (HARDWARE & SOFTWARE)

This final step in the Ten Steps to Success is, unfortunately, where most companies begin their journey to Class A MRP II. An interactive business software system in some ways is to a business what a set of golf clubs is to a golfer.

If Jack Nicklaus went golfing with you, it is unlikely that you would beat him. He has practiced and perfected his processes for years. He also has a very expensive set of golf clubs with a full complement of size and pitch. If you swapped clubs with him, would it change the outcome of the match? Our guess is that it would not. Let's think about why and how that might relate to the example of software/hardware.

The clubs are not the most important part of the process for Jack. He has disciplined himself to keep his left elbow straight and his eye on the ball. His follow through is flawless, and he shifts his weight gracefully through the swing. The fact that he swapped clubs would only mildly affect his game if at all.

Businesses have proven time and time again that excellent rounds of golf can be played with less than optimum clubs. Granted, it is difficult to play golf without clubs, but it is possible to play as long as you have some of the basic clubs. Many companies enter into an MRP II implementation misdirected into thinking that software can solve all the problems.

10 Steps to MRP Failure
or How To Do It Wrong

1) **Ignore Management Education**
   Or get it from a software or hardware vendor

2) **Do Not Get Outside Guidance**
   For project or management team

3) **Don't Evaluate Present Performance**
   To identify problem performance areas

4) **Don't Form a Project Team**
   We can do it on a part-time basis

5) **Appoint the DP Manager as Project Leader**
   Or make it a DP project

6) **Cost Justify Only the computer Hardware**
   Forget the other costs involved

7) **Don't Develop an Overall Project Plan**
   Or really get into project management with all activities loaded on the computer

8) **Concentrate on the Computer System and Loading the Data Base**
   Rather than the management system and running the business

9) **Make Software & Hardware Selection Your First Step**

10) **Start Over Again — *But This Time DO IT RIGHT!***

Figure 11-7: Ten Steps to MRP Failure

Experience has shown from our surveying, working in and working with Class A companies that approximately 25% of the benefits of MRP II might be derived from new software tools. Benefits of new software typically include:

1. System Integration

The new software is an integrated package whereas the existing company systems might be stand-alone or not fully integrated. In this situation it is not unusual for the company operating personnel to be taking data out of one system only to input it into another system.

2. Increased Functionality

Again, the new software may provide increased functionality that the current system does not provide. Typical software module areas of improvement might be forecasting and master scheduling, where as in the past these functions probably were attempted manually.

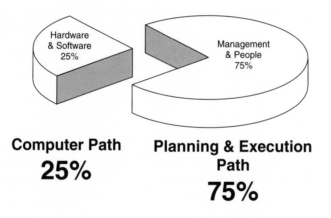

Computer Path
25%

Planning & Execution Path
75%

Figure 11-8: MRP II Benefits

To achieve 75% of the benefits of the MRP II implementation, improvements in the operating performance must transpire.

Choosing Software

There are entire books devoted to the requirements for manufacturing resource planning software and how to choose the software package that best fits a company's needs. Rather than try to duplicate that effort here, let's concentrate on important points in the selection process.

Point 1: Obviously, in reading this chapter on the Ten Steps to Success, as the reader you have discovered that Class A MRP II companies start with education and looking at their operating performance in the business before embarking on a hardware/software implementation.

Point 2: The system selection process should not be left up to information systems. They are not the real users — operations is. Therefore, involve the cross-functional project team in the selection process.

Point 3: The requirements definition should be for the whole company. Again, what functionality is required, for example, in the sales area to facilitate forecasting and a monthly update of the forecast?

Point 4: Quickly narrow the selection process to 2-3 suppliers. The first rule is to look only at suppliers who can demonstrate that their package is fully up and running in at least two business environments. Do not be fooled by how many users the software supplier says they have. They probably are including companies that have bought one module or some of the modules, not the number of companies that have fully implemented the package. If the supplier cannot provide companies that have the package fully implemented, move on.

Point 5: Do not make this phase a 12-18 month project in and of itself. Companies that spend 12-18 months typically are looking at a lot of packages (some companies as many as 50 different packages), and are wasting time.

Point 6: When narrowing the selection process talk with users of the software product. Do not just accept a glowing report from information systems: talk with the real users in operations.

Get their feedback and thoughts on the software and the company supplying the software.

Point 7: Base the selection on not just a good sales presentation by the software company. Base the selection on the functionality of the software, their training, financial health of the company and their support for the implementation. Meet the individual who will be assigned to your company account to provide training and technical support.

Implementing Software

There are two distinct schools of thought when it comes to software application in a company business environment. One side argues that there is no software product that truly meets the company's needs. "Our business is different" or "we do not operate the way the software does or is forcing us to in this area." The company purchases a software product and sets about altering the product to their current business environment. Many companies spend as much time and money altering the product as they paid for it in the first place. Experience has shown that companies typically end up modifying new software to look like the old product they just discarded. For example, screens and reports are modified at user request to change the new tool because the user is used to a particular format or screen. Another major reason for software modification is that the company does not want to address the issues the new software brings to the surface. Because it is too difficult, management does not address the questions of "how and why do we do business this way?" and so it is easier to change the software.

This is not to condone an approach where companies change their business to fit the software. What successful companies are doing, however, is looking at their operational performance and mapping business processes to identify areas of improvement. From this it can be determined how software fits and how it should be implemented. The recommendation is to think of software as a 90-95% solution. In other words, when modifications are discussed, break them into two simple categories. First, a "need to" modification. A "need to" modification is a show stopper. This basically says the project cannot move forward until this change is made. These are the modifications to discuss as a team. If the decision by the team is that the MRP II project cannot proceed then the modification probably should be made. The second category is the "nice to" modifications. These are modifications to the software that people would like to have. These types of modifications normally are due to what was discussed before — where people are used to the old screens and reports and want them back. This second category should be set aside for at least 6 months after implementation. Most of these desires will fall by the way as users become familiar with the existing screens and reports.

It also is important to understand that when the new software was purchased part of the decision set probably was due to the software supplier's stance to continue to upgrade and improve their product. Too many company modifications in this case would make it extremely difficult (time and money) to convert to the newly released upgrade or version.

From this chapter and, hopefully, throughout the entire book, it has become apparent that achieving Class A Manufacturing Resource Planning is not about implementing a new computer system. What gets and keeps companies Class A is their approach and understanding of training their people and focusing on company operating performance and business processes to drive a habit of ongoing improvement in the business enterprise.

Best wishes on your journey.

Appendix A:
Monthly Operations Review Meeting

ABC Company Monthly Operations Review Meeting

Date: 1st Monday of
New Month

Time: 9:00 AM

Place: President's Office

Attendees:

President
Mgr. Manufacturing
Mgr. Marketing
Mgr. Materials

Mgr. Engineering
Controller
Mgr. Human Resources
Master Scheduler

Agenda

I. **Review Month's Performance** (by Dollars and Units)
   A. Business Plan
   B. Shipment Plan
   C. Production Plan
   D. Inventory/Backlog/Bookings Plan

II. **Review Outlook 30-60-90-120 Days** (by Dollars and Units)
   A. Business Plan
   B. Shipment Plan
   C. Production Plan
   D. Inventory/Backlog/Bookings Plan

III. **Updated Production Plan**

Figure A-1

Last Month's Performance
By Product Line
By Units & Net Dollars

PRODUCT FAMILY	BUSINESS PLAN		SHIP PERFORMANCE						PRODUCTION		
			SHIP PLAN		SHIP ACTUAL		PERF. %		PLAN	ACTUAL	PERF.
	UNITS	$	UNITS	$	UNITS	$	UNITS	$	UNITS	UNITS	UNITS
ROTO TILLER	40	100	44	110	38	95	86	86	50	49	98
PEANUT EQUIP.	81	405	76	380	81	405	94	94	90	90	100
CULTIVATOR	31	125	31	125	34	150	91	83	40	35	88
CHISEL EQUIP.	17	51	17	51	15	38	88	74	18	18	100
PRIMARY TILL.	138	370	140	375	140	396	100	95	151	128	85
FERT. EQUIP.	34	180	30	159	32	147	94	93	30	30	100
HOE-N-TILL	208	421	200	404	210	440	95	92	205	201	98
PLANTER EQUIP.	128	705	141	776	141	776	100	100	151	118	78
NO-TILL EQUIP.	38	155	40	163	38	155	95	95	40	24	60
UNI-DRILL	14	81	12	72	12	80	100	90	14	14	100
SERVICE PARTS	–	250	–	264	–	258	–	98	–	–	–
TOTAL	729	$2843	731	$2879	741	$2940	94	91	789	707	91

Figure A-2

Last Month's Orders & Backlog
By Units & Net Dollars

PRODUCT FAMILY	BEGINNING BACKLOG		PLAN		ACTUAL		PERF. %		SHIP ACTUAL		ENDING BACKLOG	
	UNITS	$	UNITS	$	UNITS	$	UNITS	$	UNITS	$	UNITS	$
ROTO TILLER	71	148	32	87	30	80	94	92	38	95	63	133
PEANUT EQUIP.	90	441	75	375	78	370	104	99	81	405	87	406
CULTIVATOR	24	112	41	155	45	181	109	116	34	150	35	143
CHISEL EQUIP.	34	102	7	17	4	12	57	71	15	38	23	76
PRIMARY TILL.	208	517	118	312	81	708	69	66	140	396	149	329
FERT. EQUIP.	17	131	24	112	38	161	158	143	32	147	23	145
HOE-N-TILL	141	312	121	300	161	381	133	127	210	440	92	253
PLANTER EQUIP.	187	1207	110	671	107	634	97	94	141	776	153	1065
NO-TILL EQUIP.	61	208	17	55	2	12	12	22	38	155	25	65
UNI-DRILL	7	42	17	91	9	58	53	64	12	80	4	20
SERVICE PARTS	–	528	–	312	–	294	–	94	–	258	–	564
TOTAL	840	3748	562	2487	555	2891	98	86	741	2940	654	3199

Figure A-3

187

Next Month's Outlook

PRODUCT FAMILY	BUSINESS PLAN		SHIPMENT OUTLOOK		PRODUCTION PLAN	
	UNITS	$	UNITS	$	UNITS	$
ROTO TILLER	32	80	38	95	42	100
PEANUT EQUIP.	90	450	80	400	90	450
CULTIVATOR	25	102	33	121	35	131
CHISEL EQUIP.	12	36	10	30	6	18
PRIMARY TILL.	145	377	135	351	130	338
FERT. EQUIP.	40	238	28	167	30	152
HOE-N-TILL	175	370	158	345	178	402
PLANTER EQUIP.	156	858	148	814	130	725
NO-TILL EQUIP.	14	60	11	52	18	72
UNI-DRILL	12	72	12	72	14	78
SERVICE PARTS	–	306	–	300	–	300
TOTAL	701	$2949	653	$2747	673	$2766

Figure A-4

Appendix B:
Buker, Inc.
Business Excellence
Implementation

C A T E G O R Y	M I L E S T O N E	T A S K	Milestone Description	Q U A R T I L E	Plan	/ Actual
100			EDUCATION			
	10		Top Management BEC – JIT – TQM	1	_____	/ _____
	15		Operating Management BEC	1	_____	/ _____
	20		Operating Management JIT	1	_____	/ _____
	25		Operating Management TQM	1	_____	/ _____
	30		Operating Management Office Excellence	1	_____	/ _____
	35		Sales/Production Planning/Master Scheduling	1	_____	/ _____
	40		Inventory Record Accuracy	1	_____	/ _____
	45		Engineering For Excellence	1	_____	/ _____
	50		Process Mapping Course	2	_____	/ _____
	55		Project Team Video - MRP Completed	2	_____	/ _____
	60		Project Team Video - JIT Completed	2	_____	/ _____

65		Steering Comm. Video Education Completed	2	_____ / _____
70		Company Video Education Plan Created	1	_____ / _____
75		Train The Trainer	1	_____ / _____
80		Team Building/Change Management/ Process Thinking/Problem Solving Course (SGIA)	2	_____ / _____
85		Company Class A User Visit	2	_____ / _____
90		Professional Certification Process Started	2	_____ / _____
95		Ongoing Education Process Defined	2	_____ / _____

200		**PROJECT ORGANIZATION**		
10		Steering Committee Established	1	_____ / _____
	A	Role Of Steering Committee Defined		
	B	Monthly Steering Committee Meetings Started		
	C	Meeting Minutes Sent To Consultant Monthly		
15		Project Manager Selected, Full-Time	1	_____ / _____
20		Project Team Established	1	_____ / _____
	A	Role Of Project Team Understood		
	B	Weekly Project Team Meetings Started		
	C	Minutes Sent To Consultant Semi-Monthly		
25		Kick-Off Meeting Held	1	_____ / _____
30		Monthly Company Communication Process Established	1	_____ / _____
35		Small Groups Defined, Staffed, Educated	2	_____ / _____

300		**PROJECT PLAN**		
10		Objective & Goal Defined For Each Major Area	1	_____ / _____
15		Excellence Plan Created With Class A Date	1	_____ / _____
	A	MRP II Tasks Defined		
	B	JIT Tasks Defined		
	C	TQM Tasks Defined		
	D	Continuous Improvement Milestones Established		
20		Plan Review With Consultant	1	_____ / _____
25		Plan Updated Weekly, Published Monthly	1	_____ / _____
30		Excellence Commitment Statement Published	1	_____ / _____

35		Business Processes Defined And Mapped	1	____ / ____
	A	All Current "Is" Condition Processes Defined	1	____ / ____
	B	All Current "Is" Processes Mapped	1	____ / ____
	C	All Proposed "Should" Processes Defined	2	____ / ____
	D	All Proposed "Should" Processes Mapped	2	____ / ____
	E	All Proposed "Should" Processes Implemented	3/4	____ / ____

400 COST JUSTIFICATION

10	Project Justification Complete	1	____ / ____
15	Justification Approved By Steering Committee	1	____ / ____
20	Project Budget Completed And Approved	1	____ / ____

500 SOFTWARE/HARDWARE

10	Software Task Force Established	2	____ / ____
15	Software Task Force Educated	2	____ / ____
20	"Standard System" Review	2	____ / ____
25	Requirements Definition Complete (300 35 C&D)	2	____ / ____
30	Software/Hardware Selected	2	____ / ____
35	Software/Hardware Installed	2	____ / ____
40	Conference Room Pilot Plan Developed (300 35 C&D)	3	____ / ____
45	Conference Room Pilot Completed, Documented (300 35 C&D)	3	____ / ____
50	Conversion Programs Defined And Tested	3	____ / ____
55	Conversion Plan Established	3	____ / ____
60	Software Training Program Established	3	____ / ____
65	On-Going Training Program Established	4	____ / ____
70	Software Conversion Complete	4	____ / ____

600		TOP MANAGEMENT PLANNING			
10		Product Family/Lines Defined	1	_____ /	_____
	A	Planning Unit Of Measure Defined			
	B	Manufacturing Strategy Defined By Family			
15		Business Plan Established	1	_____ /	_____
	A	Mission Statement Published			
	B	Annual Budget Established			
	C	Business Objectives Established			
	D	Products And Markets Formalized			
	E	Product Profiles Completed			
	F	Long Range 3-5 Year Plan Developed			
	G	Review Policy And Procedure Established			
	H	Performance Measurement Established			
20		Sales Planning Established	1	_____ /	_____
	A	Product Line Forecast- Min. 12 Mo. Horizon			
	B	Competitive Lead Times Established			
	C	Forecast Algorithm Established			
	D	Review Policy And Procedure Established			
	E	Performance Measurement Established			
	F	Weekly Performance To Plan Tracked			
25		Production Planning Established	1	_____ /	_____
	A	Product Line Production Plan Established			
	B	Plan Is Updated Monthly			
	C	Resource Profiles Established			
	D	Manufacturing Cycle Times Documented			
	E	Review Policy And Procedure Established			
	F	Performance Measurement Established			
	G	Weekly Performance To Plan			
30		Monthly Operations Review Meeting Established	1	_____ /	_____
35		Monthly Operations Review Meeting Effective	2	_____ /	_____
40		Monthly Bookings Review Established	1	_____ /	_____
45		Monthly Bookings Review Effective	2	_____ /	_____

700		PERFORMANCE MEASUREMENT			
10		Business Performance Objectives Established	1	_____ /	_____
15		All Measurements Formally Documented	1	_____ /	_____
	A	Definition			
	B	Information Source			
	C	Owner Definition			
	D	Sample Calculation			
	E	Reporting Process			
20		Steering Committee Approves Measurements	1	_____ /	_____
25		Performance Measurement Process Started	2	_____ /	_____
	A	Top Management Measurements			
	B	Operating Management Measurements			
	C	Execution Measurements			
	D	Database Measurements			
	E	Cause Analysis Is Utilized			
	F	Monthly Performance Meeting Established			
	G	Performance Results Communicated			
30		Valid Measurements In Every Category	2	_____ /	_____
35		Continuous Improvement Measurements Defined	2	_____ /	_____
40		Continuous Improvement Measurements Started	2	_____ /	_____
45		Weekly Performance To Plan Is Utilized	1	_____ /	_____
50		Perf. History To Buker With Support Documentation	1	_____ /	_____
55		Policy/Procedure For Update/Review Of Measurements	1	_____ /	_____
60		World Class Performance Measurements Established	2	_____ /	_____
	A	Cost			
	B	Quality			
	C	Flexibility			
	D	Reliability			
	E	Innovation			
	F	Others As Defined By Company			

750		DEMAND MANAGEMENT/DISTRIBUTION		
10		Demand Manager Established	2	___ / ___
20		Distribution Strategy Reviewed	2	___ / ___

800		MASTER PRODUCTION SCHEDULING		
10		Define Item Manufacturing Strategy	2	___ / ___
15		Document MPS Change Procedure	2	___ / ___
20		Document MPS Time Fence Policy	2	___ / ___
	A	Draft MPS Time Fence Policy In Place		
	B	Define Item Time Fences (Rate, Mix, Firm)		
25		Formalized MPS/Production Plan Policy	2	___ / ___
	A	Time Fence Policies Defined		
	B	Change Policies Defined		
	C	Rules & Responsibilities Defined		
	D	Order Promising & Quoting Defined		
	E	Performance Measurements Defined		
30		Define And Document Planning Bills-Of-Material	2	___ / ___
	A	Identify MPS Items		
	B	Identify Mix Percentages		
40		MPS Implementation	2	___ / ___
	A	Pilot Approach Is Used		
	B	Manual MPS Is Utilized		
	C	100% Input Is Defined For The Family		
45		MPS And ATP Implementation	3	___ / ___
	A	MPS/OE Flow Model Is Developed		
	B	ATP Etiquette Is Defined		
50		Rough-Cut Capacity Planning	3	___ / ___
	A	Resource Profiles Developed		
	B	RCCP Etiquette Is Defined		
55		MPS Is Effective	3	___ / ___
	A	MPS Replanned Weekly/Daily		
	B	Bookings Review Includes Mix Analysis (600 30 A&B)		

	C	Weekly Mps Release Process Established			
60		Performance Measurement Process Established	2	____ /	____
65		Level Load And Balanced Flow Is Utilized	4	____ /	____
900		**DATABASE DEVELOPMENT**			
10		Owners Defined For All Master File Data Elements	2	____ /	____
	A	Item Elements Defined			
15		Item Master Files Loaded And Managed	2	____ /	____
	A	New Part Number Request Process Defined			
	B	Item Master Change Process Defined			
20		Bill-Of-Material Accuracy	2	____ /	____
	A	BOM Audit Methodology Defined			
	B	BOM Audited For Quantity, U/M, Items			
	C	BOM Reflects Manufacturing Process			
25		Engineering Change Maintenance	2	____ /	____
	A	BOM Under Engineering Change			
	B	Database Correction Within 24 Hrs Implement.			
30		Bill-Of-Material Policies And Procedures Developed	2	____ /	____
35		Inventory Record Accuracy	1	____ /	____
	A	Responsibility Defined And Understood			
	B	Inventory Flow Model Of Current Process			
	C	Inventory Flow Model Of Proposed Process			
40		Inventory Accuracy Process Implementation	2	____ /	____
	A	Proposed Model Implemented			
	B	Stockrooms Defined And Organized			
	C	Pull Systems Are Utilized			
	D	Policies And Procedures Implemented			
45		Control Group Cycle Count Program Established	2	____ /	____
50		Full Cycle Count Program Established	2	____ /	____
55		Performance Measurement Process Established	2	____ /	____
60		Routings Development	2	____ /	____

60	A	Work Centers Defined		
	B	Operations Defined		
	C	Demonstrated W/C Queue Established		
	D	Demonstrated Run/Set-Up Times Established		
65		Routings Created To Reflect Manufacturing Process	2	____ / ____
70		Routings Database Under Engineering Change Control	2	____ / ____
	A	Data Base Correction Within 24 Hrs Implement.		
75		Performance Measurement Process Established	2	____ / ____
80		Policy And Procedures Update And Review Process	2	____ / ____

1000   MATERIAL REQUIREMENTS PLANNING

10		Planning Database Defined And Updated	3	____ / ____
	A	Planner Codes		
	B	Planning L/T Equals Routing Or Supplier L/T		
	C	Lot Sizes, Multiples, Etc. Defined		
15		Weekly Order Schedule Policy And Procedure	3	____ / ____
20		All MRP Input Defined	3	____ / ____
25		Performance Measurement Process Established	3	____ / ____
30		Policy And Procedures Update And Review Process	3	____ / ____
35		Small Lot Production Plan Defined	4	____ / ____

1100   CAPACITY REQUIREMENTS PLANNING / ROUGH CUT

10		Rough Cut Capacity Planning	3	____ / ____
	A	Resource Profiles Developed		
	B	RCCP Etiquette Is Defined		
15		Demonstrated Capacity Known By Critical Resource	3	____ / ____

1200		PURCHASING		
10		Item/Supplier Database Elements Defined, Loaded	2	_____ / _____
	A	Item Lead Time		
	B	Purchase Planner Codes		
	C	Supplier Information		
15		Purchase Orders Released On System	2	_____ / _____
20		Purchase Orders Released & Updated Based On MRP	3	_____ / _____
25		Scheduled Release Is Utilized	3	_____ / _____
30		Supplier Partnership Program Developed	4	_____ / _____
35		Performance Measurement Process Established	1	_____ / _____
40		Policy And Procedures Update And Review Process	2	_____ / _____
1300		SHOP FLOOR EXECUTION		
10		Daily Priority Planning	3	_____ / _____
	A	Operation Status Is Utilized		
	B	Daily Dispatch List Is Utilized		
	C	Daily Meeting With Supervisors And Planners		
15		Setup Reduction Plan Developed	2	_____ / _____
20		Structured Flow Is Utilized	2	_____ / _____
25		Housekeeping Plan Developed	2	_____ / _____
30		Control Through Visible Means Is Utilized	2	_____ / _____
35		Small Group Improvement Activities Are Utilized	2	_____ / _____
40		Preventative Maintenance Program Developed	2	_____ / _____
45		Cycle Time Reduction Program Established	3	_____ / _____
50		Production Workers Responsible For Their Own Quality	1	_____ / _____
55		Material Flow Process Defined	2	_____ / _____
60		Performance Measurement Process Established	2	_____ / _____
65		Policy And Procedures Update And Review Process	3	_____ / _____

1400	FINANCIAL			
10	Review And Audit The Inventory Flow Process	2	_____ / _____
15	Requirements For Physical Inventory Elimination	4	_____ / _____
20	Operations Generate Financial Results	3	_____ / _____
25	Define Costing Based On The Operations	4	_____ / _____
30	Map The AP/AR/Gl/Payroll Processes	4	_____ / _____
35	Define/Update Policies/Procedures	4	_____ / _____
40	Reduce Cost-Added Activities By 50%	4	_____ / _____

1500	QUALITY			
10	Facilitate Small Group Improvement Activity Process	2	_____ / _____
15	Facilitate Fitness For Use Culture Change	1	_____ / _____
20	Supplier Certification Process Plan Developed	4	_____ / _____
25	Facilitate Outside Quality Improvements	4	_____ / _____
30	Compliance To Government Regulations	2	_____ / _____
35	Class A Readiness Review	4	_____ / _____
40	Class A Audit By Buker, Inc.	4	_____ / _____

1600	HUMAN RESOURCES			
10	Set Up And Administer Video Education	1	_____ / _____
15	Conduct Train The Trainer Course	2	_____ / _____
20	Job Descriptions Reflect Process Improvement/Performance Criteria	4	_____ / _____
25	Publish The Results/Story	4	_____ / _____
30	Company Library Defined And Established	2	_____ / _____

1700	CONTINUOUS IMPROVEMENT			
10	Performance Measurement Criteria Tightened	4	_____ / _____
15	Execution Measurements Redefined	4	_____ / _____
20	Plan Established To Reduce Transactions By 50%	4	_____ / _____
25	Vision For The Future Statement Published	4	_____ / _____
30	Continuous Improvement Audit Process Defined	4	_____ / _____

Appendix C:
Sample Project Plan

ABC COMPANY OPERATIONAL EXCELLENCE PLAN

A. TEAM MISSION STATEMENT: OPERATIONAL EXCELLENCE TEAM

To guide the organization to a level of basic business excellence where there is a one plan process, and all functions are integrated through the formal new business system. To accomplish this task, it is understood that in all business areas performance must be a minimum of 95% performance.

Upon completion of the one plan process being established with at least 95% performance in each business area, the responsibility of the operational excellence team will be to begin to move the organization to a process of continuous improvement leading to operational excellence.

By accomplishing these goals we will position our corporation to operate with the highest level of reliability, flexibility, competitiveness and responsiveness possible for total internal and external customer satisfaction.

1. TOP MANAGEMENT PLANNING

Objective:

To define by division, product lines and families for business, sales and production planning purposes and their respective manufacturing strategies. This will allow detail business plans to be developed. Product lines and families along with the manufacturing strategy should be reviewed on an annual basis.

	TASKS	START DATE	COMPLETION DATE	RESPONSIBILITY
1A	Product lines/families reviewed by division	2/12/xx	4/01/xx	Division Mgrs Finance Plant Mgrs Sales
1B)	Mfg. strategy defined by family (MTS, MTO, ATO, ETO)	2/26/xx	4/15/xx	Plant Mgrs OPS Mgrs Division Mgrs Sales
1C)	Develop a pilot one plan process to be reviewed by executive management, division manager, sales manager and finance	4/01/xx	5/01/xx	Team

2. BUSINESS PLAN

Objective:

To develop an annual business plan for ABC Company defined by division and product line (see Section 1). The annual plan should be developed in net sales dollars and unit of measure by month and by product line. The plan should have financial considerations as well as sales considerations. This can be done for as short a period as one year and up to five years. The plan should be reviewed on a monthly basis and updated annually.

	TASKS	START DATE	COMPLETION DATE	RESPONSIBILITY
2A)	Business plan documented and defined by division and by product line (units and dollars) by month	2/12/xx	4/01/xx	CEO VP Sales CFO Division Mgrs
2B)	Process developed for update of business plan by divisions	2/26/xx	4/01/xx	CEO VP Sales CFO Division Mgrs

3. SALES/DEMAND PLAN

Objective:

To develop by division and product line an overall rate of anticipated demand expressed in dollars and unit of measure and broken into monthly buckets allowing for a monthly review of bookings to plan. It should be reviewed and updated on a monthly basis.

TASKS		START DATE	COMPLETION DATE	RESPONSIBILITY
3A)	Division forecast by product line in dollars and units by month	2/19/xx	6/01/xx	VP Sales Demand Mgmt
3B)	Forecast developed with 12 month horizon with monthly updated by division	2/19/xx	6/01/xx	VP Sales Demand Mgmt
3C)	Finished goods inventory levels established by product and product line division	2/19/xx	6/01/xx	Division Mgrs Plant Mgrs VP Sales Demand Mgmt
3D)	Monthly bookings review established by divisions to review forecast accuracy monthly	6/01/xx	7/01/xx	Demand Mgmt Division Mgrs Plant Mgrs OPS Mgrs Planning/ Scheduling VP Sales
3E)	Achieve 95% performance to the forecast by product line by month	6/01/xx	12/31/xx	VP Sales Demand Mgmt

4. PRODUCTION PLANNING

Objective:

To develop by division and product line the production rates and resources needed to meet the sales plan. The production plan also will provide the basis for management control through the process of inventory objectives and delivery expectations. It should be reviewed and updated on a monthly basis.

	TASKS	START DATE	COMPLETION DATE	RESPONSIBILITY
4A)	Divisional production plans developed by product line in dollars and unit of measure by month	4/01/xx	6/15/xx	Plant Mgrs OPS Mgrs Finance (plant)
4B)	Production plan developed with 12-month horizons with monthly update by divisions	4/01/xx	6/15/xx	Plant Mgrs OPS Mgrs
4C)	Performance to production plan reviewed	4/01/xx	12/31/xx	Plant Mgrs OPS Mgrs
4D)	Achieve 95% performance by product line to the production plan	4/01/xx	7/01/xx	Plant Mgrs OPS Mgr
4E)	Develop monthly operations review by division to review business, sales and product plan performance	4/01/xx	7/01/xx	Plant Mgrs OPS Mgrs Finance VP Sales Division Mgrs Demand Mgmt

5. MASTER PRODUCTION SCHEDULE

Objective:

To provide the link between top management planning and the day to day operating plans. The master production schedule should interpret monthly production requirements into weekly schedules. It should be defined at the item level and be reviewed and updated on a weekly, or even daily, basis.

	TASKS	START DATE	COMPLETION DATE	RESPONSIBILITY
5A)	Establish an education plan pertaining to planning bills consisting of specific software issues and general planning bill logic	3/13/xx	9/01/xx	OPS Mgr Planning
5B)	Develop pilot planning bills by product line for each division	3/07/xx	4/01/xx	OPS Mgr Planning
5C)	Develop planning bills of material/capacity by product line and division	3/07/xx	4/15/xx	OPS Mgr Demand Mgmt Planning
5D)	Develop percentages for use in planning bills by product line by division	3/07/xx	4/15/xx	OPS Mgr. Planning
5E)	Develop summarized routings for rough cut capacity by product line and divisions	3/07/xx	8/01/xx	OPS Mgr Planning
5F)	Policies and procedures defined for master schedule change, time fences	4/01/xx	8/01/xx	OPS Mgr Planning
5G)	Establish master schedule items for use in software system by division	6/15/xx	8/15/xx	OPS Mgr Planning Info Systems
5H)	Convert all product lines to master scheduling for each division	8/01/xx	9/01/xx	OPS Mgr Planning Order Entry

5I)	Establish procedure for daily update and running of MPS	8/01/xx	9/01/xx	OPS Mgr Sales
5J)	Implement ATP planning logic for use by planning and order entry	9/01/xx	11/01/xx	OPS Mgr Planning Order Entry
5K)	Weekly review and update process established for MPS	8/01/xx	9/01/xx	OPS Mgr Planning Order Entry
5L)	Achieve 95% of performance to the MPS by week	8/01/xx	12/31/xx	OPS Mgr Planning

6. DATA BASE

Objective:

To provide the highest level of data integrity in all pertinent data files such as:

> Bills of Material 99%+
> Routings 99%
> Inventory Status 99%

These files interface with all aspects of the business: without this level of accuracy the business plans cannot be executed.

	TASKS	START DATE	COMPLETION DATE	RESPONSIBILITY
6A)	Bills of material develop audit methodology for bills of material	3/04/xx	3/11/xx	Engineering OPS Mgr Finance
6B)	Begin audit of bills of material utilizing audit methodology	4/06/xx	7/31/xx	Engineering
6C)	Develop method for quick turnaround on bills of material errors (24-hour turnaround)	4/06/xx	4/30/xx	Engineering
6D)	Achieve 99% record integrity on bills of material	4/06/xx	7/31/xx	
6E)	Develop audit methodology for routings	3/04/xx	3/27/xx	Manufacturing Engineering OPS Mgr Finance
6F)	Begin audit of routings utilizing audit methodology	4/06/xx	4/30/xx	Manufacturing Engineering
6G)	Develop method for quick turnaround on routings (24-hour turnaround); achieve 99% record integrity on routings	4/06/xx	4/30/xx	Manufacturing Engineering

6H)	Inventory accuracy: define cycle count methodology by division	3/04/xx	3/27/xx	OPS Mgr
6I)	Begin control group cycle count & publish & post results formally	4/06/xx	6/26/xx	OPS Mgr
6J)	Implement full cycle count program	7/01/xx	12/31/xx	OPS Mgr
6K)	Develop policy and procedure for count error analysis and reconciliation	4/06/xx	6/26/xx	OPS Mgr
6L)	Achieve 98% record integrity on inventory	11/30/xx	12/31/xx	OPS Mgr
6M)	Eliminate physical inventory	11/30/xx	12/31/94	OPS Mgr

7. MATERIAL REQUIREMENTS PLANNING

Objective:

To provide the actual plan at the detail item number level of how much material and in what priority sequence to order and to satisfy the master schedule. This will create action messages that will drive the manufacturing and purchasing schedules.

TASKS		START DATE	COMPLETION DATE	RESPONSIBILITY
7A)	Determine application of MRP by division	4/01/xx	7/01/xx	OPS Mgr
7B)	Review and define data elements to support MRP application (lot sizes, minimum balance, order policy, safety stock, planner codes, item types, etc.)	7/01/xx	9/01/xx	OPS Mgr
7C)	Develop pilot product line for MRP run by divisions for those not on MRP today	7/01/xx	9/01/xx	OPS Mgr
7D)	Convert all product lines to MRP by divisions where application defined in 7A	7/01/xx	10/01/xx	OPS Mgr
7E)	Policies and procedures defined for weekly/daily update of MRP planning run	8/01/xx	12/31/xx	OPS Mgr Planning Info Systems
7F)	Achieve 95%+ performance in MRP (release and schedule reliability)	7/01/xx	12/31/xx	OPS Mgr Planning

8. PURCHASING

Objective:

To obtain the highest quality material, at the optimum value. The objective will be to develop supplier partnerships that result in 95–99% on-time delivery performance.

TASKS	START DATE	COMPLETION DATE	RESPONSIBILITY
8A) Establish a formal process for review and update of item analysis (lead times, lots, etc.)	7/01/xx	9/01/xx	Purchasing QC
8B) Develop supplier partnership program to include supplier certification	6/01/xx	10/01/xx	OPS Mgr Purchasing QC
8C) Develop pilot program for implementation with key suppliers (5-10)	10/01/xx	11/30/xx	Purchasing OPS Mgr QC
8D) Establish a formal process for review and update of purchase standards for annual update	10/01/xx	11/30/xx	Manufacturing Cost Mgr Materials Mgr
8E) Achieve 95%+ on-time performance for purchased materials (to the day)	7/01/xx	12/31/xx	Purchasing

9. MANUFACTURING PROCESSES/JIT PRINCIPLES

Objective:

To achieve a responsive production environment. The focus will be on flexibility, dependability and on-time performance driving toward a paperless environment.

TASKS	START DATE	COMPLETION DATE	RESPONSIBILITY
9A) Review of manufacturing process by division for flow and throughput (must entail process mapping or flow charting)	4/06/xx	10/01/xx	OPS Mgr Plant Mgr
9B) Develop plans for factory simplification (factory refacilitation) by division	10/01/xx	12/31/xx	OPS Mgr Plant Mgr Mfg Engineer
9C) Begin pilot product line for flow, housekeeping, preventative maintenance, and data collection	10/01/xx	12/31/xx	OPS Mgr Plant Mgr Mfg Engineer
9D) Develop housekeeping and establish organization plan with procedures for time allowed daily as well as recognition and reward	10/01/xx	12/31/xx	OPS Mgr Plant Mgr Mfg Engineer
9E) Develop preventative maintenance program and pilot for activities to be performed daily, weekly and monthly by operators; checklist identified for daily use	10/01/xx	12/31/xx	OPS Mgr. Plant Manager Mfg Engineer
9F) Setup and cycle time reductions programs activated by product line and divisions	10/01/xx	12/31/xx	OPS Mgr Plant Mgr Mfg Engineer
9G) Pilot product lines identified for pull system activities	12/15/xx	12/31/xx	OPS Mgr

9H)	Appropriate product lines converted to pull system method of production	12/15/xx	12/31/xx	OPS Mgr
9I)	Achieve schedule performance on a daily basis of 95%+	7/01/xx	12/31/xx	OPS Mgr

10. PERFORMANCE MEASUREMENT

Objective:

To define and measure the key operating areas to successfully measure the operations of the ABC Company — the operating performance measures should be reported by division

TASKS	START DATE	COMPLETION DATE	RESPONSIBILITY
10A) Define key operating performance measurements by division and business in total	3/06/xx	4/01/xx	Division Mgr Plant Mgr VP Mfg VP Operations Executive Team
10B) Define performance measurement criteria for forecast accuracy	4/01/xx	6/01/xx	Division Mgr Demand Mgr Sales Mgr
10C) Define performance measurement criteria for production plan accuracy	4/01/xx	6/15/xx	Plant Mgr
10D) Define performance measurement criteria for master schedule accuracy	4/01/xx	8/01/xx	Plant Mgr OPS Mgr
10E) Define performance measurement for material requirements accuracy	4/01/xx	9/01/xx	OPS Mgr
10F) Define inventory record accuracy measurement	3/06/xx	4/01/xx	OPS Mgr
10G) Define bill of material accuracy measurement	3/06/xx	4/01/xx	Engineering OPS Mgr
10H) Define routing accuracy measurement	3/06/xx	4/06/xx	OPS Mgr Manufacturing Engineering

10I)	Define performance measurement for purchasing on time performance and PPV	4/01/xx	7/01/xx	Purchasing
10J)	Define performance measurement for on time production performance	4/01/xx	7/01/xx	OPS Mgr
10K)	Define performance measurement for customer satisfaction			Division Mgr Plant Mgr Sales
10L)	Establish key measurement for ongoing rates of improvement: Setup Quality Cycle Time Productivity Value Added	4/01/xx	10/01/xx	Plant Mgr
10M)	Order processing cycle time/accuracy and pricing	4/01/xx	8/01/xx	
10N)	Financial measures	4/01/xx	9/01/xx	

11. TRAINING/EDUCATION

Objective:

To provide a plan that ensures that 100% of our employees have on-going training in MRP, JIT and software principles. This is at all levels of the corporation and should be made a permanent part of each employee's personnel record.

TASKS	START DATE	COMPLETION DATE	RESPONSIBILITY
11A) Develop and prioritize a corporate plan to manage and facilitate a formal education and training process	4/01/xx	7/01/xx	
11B) Benchmark high performance companies to establish employee hour/training ration (50-75 hours per)	3/07/xx	4/24/xx	
11C) Develop by division a video-based education plan to educate 100% of the workforce in MRP and JIT principles as it applies to function and need	3/04/xx	4/01/xx	Plant Mgr
11D) Conduct two day education experience for management and others in key staff/support functions	3/06/xx	4/15/xx	Plant Mgr
11E) Conduct education for senior management – sales, division managers	3/09/xx	12/31/xx	Consultant

Selected Bibliography

Bardwick, Judith M.
>   *Danger in the Comfort Zone*
>   New York, NY: American Management Association, 1991

Crosby, Philip B.
>   *Quality is Free*
>   New York, NY: McGraw Hill, 1979

Fogarty, Donald W., and Thomas R. Hoffmann
>   *Production and Inventory Management*
>   Cincinnati, OH: South Western Publishing Company, 1983

Ford, Henry
>   *Today and Tomorrow*
>   Garden City, NY: Doubleday Page & Company, 1926

Goldratt, Eliyahu, and Jeff Cox
>   *The Goal*
>   Croton-on-Hudson, NY: North River Press, 1986

Greene, James H.
>   *Production and Inventory Control Handbook*
>   New York, NY: McGraw-Hill, 1987

Grieco, Peter L. Jr., and Michael Gozzo
>   *Made In America*
>   Plantsville, CT: PT Publications, 1987

Gunn, Thomas G.
>   *Manufacturing for Competitive Advantage*
>   Cambridge, MA: Ballinger Publishing Company, 1987

Hall, Robert W.
   Attaining Manufacturing Excellence
   Homewood, IL: Dow Jones-Irwin/APICS Series in Production
   Management, 1987

Izzo, Joseph E.
   The Embattled Fortress
   San Francisco, CA: Jossey Bass Inc., 1987

Juran, J.M., editor-in-chief and Frank Gryna, assoc. ed.
   Juran's Quality Control Handbook: Fourth Edition
   New York, NY: McGraw-Hill Book Company, 1988

Mackenzie, Alec
   The Time Trap
   New York, NY: American Management Association, 1990

Orlicky, Joseph
   MRP Material Requirements Planning
   New York, NY: McGraw-Hill, 1975

Peters, Thomas J.
   In Search of Excellence
   New York, NY: Warner Books, 1982

Schonberger, Richard J.
   Japanese Manufacturing Techniques
   New York, NY: Macmillan Press, 1982

Shingo, Shigeo
   The Sayings of Shigeo Shingo
   Cambridge, MA: Productivity Press, 1987

Suzaki, Kiyoshi
   The New Manufacturing Challenge
   New York, NY: Macmillan, Inc., 1987

Turcotte, Edward
   "Total Quality, Not A Program: It's a Way of Life"
   Journey. Volume 3, Number 2. Quarter 2 (1992): 8-9
   Antioch, IL: Buker, Inc., 1992

Tzu, Sun and James Clavell
   The Art of War
   New York, NY: Delacorte Press, 1983

Walton, Mary
    The Deming Management Method
    New York, NY: Putnam Publishing, 1986

Vollmann, Thomas E., William Lee Berry, and D.Clay Whybark
    Manufacturing Planning and Control Systems
    Homewood, IL: Dow Jones-Irwin/APICS Series in Production
    Management, 1988